THE POWER TO COMPETE

THE POWER TO COMPETE

An Economist and an Entrepreneur on Revitalizing Japan in the Global Economy

Hiroshi Mikitani
Ryoichi Mikitani

WILEY

Cover image: Hiroshi Noguchi
Cover design: Seiichi Suzuki

Published by John Wiley & Sons, Inc., Hoboken, New Jersey.
Published simultaneously in Canada.

For general information about our other products and services, please contact our Customer Care
Department within the United States at (800) 762-2974, outside the United States at (317) 572-3993
or fax (317) 572-4002.

Wiley publishes in a variety of print and electronic formats and by print-on-demand. Some
material included with standard print versions of this book may not be included in e-books or in
print-on-demand. If this book refers to media such as a CD or DVD that is not included in the
version you purchased, you may download this material at http://booksupport.wiley.com.
For more information about Wiley products, visit www.wiley.com.

ISBN 978-1-119-00060-0 (cloth);
ISBN 978-1-119-00114-0 (ebk);
ISBN 978-1-119-00115-7 (ebk)

Printed in the United States of America
10 9 8 7 6 5 4 3 2

Contents

Introduction

Japan Again

We are in a worldwide period of tremendous change, driven by the global information technology (IT) revolution. But not all of Japan has embraced the transformation. The sad truth is that few Japanese political, business, or governmental leaders understand where we are and where we are going. In many important ways, Japan today is the same as it was in the Edo period, when our country was closed off to the world and the leaders of the *shogunate*[1] paid no mind to the changes happening abroad.

Even though we are seeing massive global changes in the IT industry, Japan as a whole seems unable to participate in the process. We drift aimlessly. The IT revolution has created structural shifts that are bringing the world together as if it were one continent. And yet, in Japan, people continue to prefer conventional frameworks, believing that we should enjoy a separate, isolated kind of Galapagos island. People here

---

[1]This was the Japanese feudal government headed by a shogun in the Edo period (1603–1868).

do not even try to consider the current global reality. This is as true for cell phones as it is for corporate governance and international accounting standards. I believe that the old guard's refusal to allow society to change only results in lowered productivity and weaker competitiveness for Japan.

Nowhere is this problem more obvious than in our government bureaucracy, which has become so bloated and rigid that it should really be called state capitalism. The continuation of the bureaucracy-led economy can only create a situation in which innovation is stifled; it will not inspire economic growth. And as the Japanese economy decelerates, the national debt continues to swell. It is difficult to imagine that this country has a future if we maintain the current spiral of loss in which the public is forced to swallow tax increases just so the government can somehow get by.

Japan is a country of rich traditions, culture, and philosophies cultivated over a 2,000-year history. We also excel in advanced technology and creativity. We need to share this intellectual and technical wealth. We must not limit our ambitions to our own small national borders and become a country of exclusion. Japan should instead become a country of greater openness, one that accepts a variety of people and cultures, and is attractive to people everywhere. This calls for two intertwined goals: (1) We must work to become the wealthiest country in the world; and (2) we must also strive to become a safe and peaceful country with highly advanced science, technology, and culture.

My work with the Japan Association of New Economy is aimed at achieving those goals. First, we must eliminate anachronistic regulations. At the same time, we must develop innovative businesses and services through the use of the Internet and other IT, and connect that innovation to the economic growth of Japan.

The second Abe[2] administration, inaugurated in December 2012, created three councils—the Council on Economic and Fiscal Policy, the Industrial Competitiveness Council, and the Regulatory Reform Council—to act as the "control towers" for the economic revitalization plan popularly called Abenomics.[3] As a member of the Industrial Competitiveness Council, I have had the opportunity to debate a growth strategy, the third arrow of Abenomics. I combined my thoughts as a business leader on that debate into a proposal entitled "Japan Again."

While working on these issues of government and growth strategies, it occurred to me that I wanted to write a book about the topic. And I knew early on whom I would ask to be my coauthor: my father. My dad, an economist and a professor emeritus at Kobe University, had often been my debate partner and sounding board as I explored issues around the Japanese economy. He passed away in late 2013, but before that happened, we engaged in a series of discussions about the future of Japan and the global economy. The result of those debates is this book. My father was instrumental in helping me to understand where we are now, what has led us to this place, and what we must do going forward for Japan and for the larger global economy. It is my honor to share that thinking with you here, in the hopes of continuing the important global conversation he and I started.

Allow me to take a moment to introduce my dad: Ryoichi Mikitani was born at the start of the global economic crisis of 1929 in Nada-ku, Kobe. After graduating from the Graduate School of Economics at Kobe University, then called Kobe

---

[2]Abe is Shinzō Abe, the 57th (2006–2007) and current Prime Minister of Japan, serving as the second Abe cabinet since December 2012.
[3]Abenomics consists of three arrows: (1) a massive fiscal stimulus measure, (2) more aggressive monetary easing from the Bank of Japan, and (3) a growth strategy by structural reforms to boost Japan's competitiveness.

University of Economics, he chose the path of researcher, and from 1972 until his compulsory retirement as a public employee in 1993, he was a professor in the Graduate School of Economics at Kobe University. He specialized in financial theory and U.S. economic theory, and he served as president of the Japan Society of Monetary Economics. From there, he moved to the faculty of economics in the Graduate School of Economics at Kobe Gakuin University. He retired in 2002.

My dad was an international economist, which is a rare occupation in Japan. He studied at a language school in his teens, and he was fluent in both English and German. He easily passed the test for the Fulbright Scholar Program, which is known to be a difficult trial, and in 1959, at the age of 29, he entered the Graduate School of Arts and Sciences of Harvard University in the United States. There he studied U.S. economics, then a cutting-edge subject, and he also grew close with James Duesenberry, who was famous for his work on the demonstration effect, as well as Paul Sweezy, known as a Keynesian economist who was well versed in Marxian economics. At the same time, my dad immersed himself in tomes such as the Chinese military text *The Art of War* and *The Analects of Confucius*, becoming well versed in both Western and Eastern philosophy. The depth of his knowledge was absolutely amazing. I continue to have nothing but respect for the profundity of his insight and ability to see things for what they are. It may be more appropriate to introduce him as a philosopher or intellectual rather than as an economist.

Now for a few words about me: I was an unruly child and never one to get good grades, but my dad never had an unkind word for me. Even when I transferred out of my private junior high school after finding it difficult to fit in, he respected my feelings and supported me. Many times, when I found myself at a personal crossroads—when I graduated from Hitotsubashi University and was unsure about whether

I wanted to go into research or become a businessman; when I quit my job at the Industrial Bank of Japan [currently Mizuho Bank]; when I founded Rakuten; when I tried to buy Tokyo Broadcasting System (TBS)—I always visited my dad in Kobe to hear his suggestions. Like my wife has been, my dad was a long behind-the-scenes counselor to me as I faced important decisions in life.

If he had been a traditional parent, I suppose that I could have expected advice like "Stop trying to do things differently from other people." But Dad always supported me, telling me that if I believed something to be essentially correct, I must do it. Naturally, he always reminded me that if I was going to do something, I had better do it right.

As an entrepreneur, I am the sort of person who prefers to understand things in an intuitive way and make top-down decisions. I have previously referred to the process by which I make decisions as a game of catch between my left and right brain. When I started to feel intuitively that I was going to do something, I would go and play this game of intellectual catch with Dad. I would listen to his rational way of thinking and his questions about what my ideal outcome would be and what my experiences in the past had been like and, in the end, I always felt that I was able to transform my intuition into a feeling of certainty.

My parents were living close to me, so I could go ask for Dad's opinion whenever I wanted. But I knew I could not expect him to act as my counselor forever. He was 83 when I approached him to work on this book with me. I thought long and hard about our grand theme this time—the future of Japan—and then I asked my dad for his opinion on my ideas. In total, I had 17 different conversations covering a broad range of topics with Dad, starting in April 2013 and continuing for the following seven months. He passed away on November 9, 2013.

As we worked together on this book, it was our hope that it would help people to recognize the current difficult situation faced by Japan, as well as offer a vision for a brighter future and a road map to get there. Even as I grew up and remained close to him as an adult, there were many times when I did not fully understand what Dad's job as an economist entailed. The debates we had, for me, produced a series of revelations. We spent a lot of very valuable time together.

And so before I close, I want to emphasize the deep gratitude I feel toward my dad, my mom, and my entire family. Because Dad was not in good health toward the end of our conversations, he was joined each time by my mom, Setsuko, who helped us in various ways, including preparing documents for the meetings and organizing things. I am indebted to them all. Please enjoy the book we prepared together.

Hiroshi Mikitani
Chairman and CEO
Rakuten, Inc.
August 2014

1 | The Power to Innovate

Japan Again

Hiroshi Mikitani ("Hiroshi"): Let's talk about the theme of these conversations. I want to talk to you about why the Japanese economy has seen such persistent stagnation, and what we should do to revive it. But first, how are you feeling? How is your health?

Professor Emeritus Ryoichi Mikitani ("Ryoichi"): Oh, it's all right, I suppose. I'm in a relatively good shape. I'm really happy that I can talk with you about the Japanese economy like this. I'm looking forward to it.

Hiroshi: For the past half a year [early 2013], I have been serving as a member of the Industrial Competitiveness Council, one of the three Abenomics control towers, and I have been participating in the debate there on Japanese economic growth. We announced our compiled growth

1

strategy in June 2013. At that time, I also created a document, as best I could, to serve as a starting point for discussion—a proposal that I called "Japan Again." In that proposal, I wrote from my perspective as a business leader about what sort of growth strategy I would create if it were all up to me.

Ryoichi: It must have been quite a lot of work. I saw the news on television and read about it in the newspapers with great interest.

Hiroshi: Prime Minister Abe's original idea was that there would be four members on the council from the private sector, but in the end a total of ten were appointed. I have the suspicion that behind this was an intention on the part of the government bureaucracy to increase the number of people on the council, appoint more people with differing opinions, and thereby dilute the arguments of the private-sector side.

Ryoichi: So there was conflict between the bureaucracy and private-sector members?

Hiroshi: In the beginning, I believe that Prime Minister Abe wanted the council to work with unusual resolve. But there was the strong sense that it was all being led by the government bureaucracy. In the end, we had a free exchange of opinions, but there was not really the mind-set that we were out to produce radical policies. The main scenarios we talked about were ones for which the bureaucracy or Ministry of Economy, Trade and Industry (METI) led the way, with the private sector serving only to complement the members from the government bureaucracy.

Ryoichi: So the proposals were toned down.

Hiroshi: Yes, and as a result, some of our greatest challenges remain. One of the causes of the stagnation of the Japanese economy is industrial policy led by the government bureaucracy, which doesn't do anything except stifle competitiveness in the private sector. Look at any of the industries that METI has gotten involved in—every one of them has been ruined. I believe that the government need only create platforms for industry; there is no need for the government to set industrial policy. Regulation is fundamentally a bad thing. I want to move steadily forward with regulatory reform.

Ryoichi: I don't think that the issue is so simple as to be able to say that "regulation is bad," but I do believe that we must move forward with regulatory reform.

Hiroshi: Another cause behind the stagnation of the Japanese economy is the lack of sufficient managerial power. Look at the inventions of the DVD or fiber-optic cable: Japanese companies have superior technological capabilities. Our problem is corporate leadership. The biggest problem right now is how to enhance the power of management.

For example, take the Industrial Bank of Japan [now known as Mizuho Bank after merging with Fuji Bank and Dai-ichi Kangyo Bank], which was originally the main bank of Nissan Motors. The bank sent the management over to Nissan and tried to reform it, but nothing worked. And then Carlos Ghosn was hired as CEO, and Nissan completely turned around. The same can be said about Apple. When the company brought back Steve Jobs, it was at the brink of death, but as CEO, Jobs succeeded in a remarkable revival. In other words, it is all about who is leading a company. I think we need to remind ourselves of that.

Ryoichi: The revival at Nissan was definitely a surprise.

Hiroshi: That is why I indicated at the Industrial Competitiveness Council that we needed to bring in more managers who had achieved a corporate revival using bold ideas, as well as more of the young managers who are running leading companies.

Ryoichi: By the way, I know that you are acting as representative director of an economic group, the Japan Association of New Economy (JANE), but how does that differ from Keidanren?[1]

Hiroshi: JANE is centered on the companies and venture/start-up firms that have developed Japan's e-business and IT industries. We have already been joined by more than 600 companies. We are an economic group that aims to contribute to the development of the Japanese economy through the creation of diverse new industries. We stand in opposition to state-led industrial policies that only protect vested interests. And in that sense, we are the opposite of Keidanren. We do not promote policies that will protect conventional Japanese industries. Instead, we encourage innovation, the reform of Japan's industrial structure, and boosting our economic metabolism. We are creating policy proposals to encourage the continued creation of the entrepreneurs who are needed to develop new industries. And we continue to work toward the realization of a more global and open marketplace through regulatory reform.

The Keys to Revitalizing Japan

Hiroshi: I want to talk about what would be the keys to reviving Japan and what the options are. I proposed five factors in my proposal, "Japan Again":

1. Efficiency of the country
2. Innovation capability

---

[1]Keidanren (abbreviation of Keizai Dantai Rengokai, or Japan Business Federation in English) is known as one of the most powerful Japanese economic organizations. Established in 1946, it now has about 1,300 major Japanese companies advising the Japanese government on policy related to its member industries.

3. Operation capability
4. Global expansion and market capability
5. Brand power

I believe that economic growth means the creation of innovation.

Ryoichi: Joseph Schumpeter said that innovation means new connections. He believed that economic growth came about through the combination of new things.

Hiroshi: If that is true, then we need to create an environment in which innovation can occur. With innovation comes the birth of new markets and economic growth. The elimination of regulations is crucial to this goal. At the Industrial Competitiveness Council, I proposed the IT autobahn concept as an initiative symbolizing these ideas. Just like the German autobahn, which has no tolls or speed limits, my idea calls for the construction of the world's fastest and cheapest communications infrastructure.

The next important factor is operation capability. As the labor market solidifies, we are reaching a point in which corporations are finding it impossible to let go of old workers and hire new ones. We obviously need to hire more women, but that alone won't be enough to solve our labor shortage. We need to go further to relax dismissal regulations and promote the fluidity of the labor market. We also need to introduce a white-collar exemption that would free white-collar workers from restrictions related to the amount of hours they work. And at the same time as we do all of that, I believe we should hire more foreign nationals in fields like nursing and child care.

Ryoichi: The reality today is that the lifetime employment system that was once so prevalent in Japan has now broken down. I think many people are questioning how we should make better use of the people we hire and what our response to the new situation should be.

Hiroshi: But let's look at the big picture—we could talk about a few ways to increase competitiveness. One solution is to increase the efficiency of the state. I think we need to consider how to reform the high-cost structure of the government. If it were a corporation, increased management efficiency would mean cutting headquarters expenses such as personnel and administrative costs. Similarly, if we think of the government as being the headquarters of the entire country, I think we must reduce administrative costs through the full use of IT.

Ryoichi: The United Kingdom at one time suffered from what was called the British disease, through which the state had led the steel manufacturing industry into a slump. I fear that we are now seeing the emergence of the Japanese disease, caused by the continued promotion of misguided policies. But there is little sense of a crisis among the Japanese public. The prognosis is poor if you do not even realize that you have a disease.

Hiroshi: Related to that, I also believe there is a need for global expansion and management capability. I think people realize that our televisions, mobile phones, and other consumer electronics have undergone a kind of Galapagos effect, in which they have moved away from international standards. But personally I don't think that this applies just to electronics. We see the Galapagos effect, in which we are isolated from the world, in other areas of our society. The decrease in the number of students studying abroad and trends in the number of foreign companies setting up headquarters in Japan are astounding. Rakuten started to make English our official language in 2010, and we completely switched over in July 2012. I believe the move toward English should be happening on a national level. It is crucial that we continue efforts to create an environment that is easier for foreign nationals and foreign companies to work in.

Ryoichi: On that point, the role of journalism is very important. I don't believe we can really say that Japan is producing journalists who hold their own opinions and have an international mind-set. I also think that universities and the academic world bear a heavy responsibility for that.

Hiroshi: The last factor I want to mention is brand power. The branding of products is definitely important, but what is really crucial is the excess earning power created by the Made in Japan brand. The brand power factor asks us to consider how we can enhance that brand.

These are not small changes I've suggested. In order to eliminate regulation and promote innovation, we must completely change the entire structure of Japan. But how should we do that? I proposed key performance indicators (KPIs) to answer that question. This management method sets quantitative metrics for each issue of concern and continuously reevaluates when and to what extent those metrics are being achieved.

Ryoichi: Prime Minister Abe has recently been using the term *KPI* a lot. It may be that this was your proposal's biggest contribution to the Industrial Competitiveness Council.

Keidanren's Raison D'être

Ryoichi: Hearing your explanation, I began to wonder about Keidanren. During the period of high-speed economic growth, economic groups like Keidanren were a positive force. But when that period ended, we also began to see their negative side. Well, that is just my opinion. What do you think? Would it have been better if Keidanren didn't exist during the period of high-speed economic growth?

Hiroshi: I do believe that Keidanren has brought many issues to the government and produced certain results that have contributed to the growth of the Japanese economy. But as industrial structure has dramatically changed, we've seen the emergence of Internet services. We've seen the steady expansion of globalization, but I don't feel that they have produced frameworks that are well suited to produce innovation powered by these new trends.

Ryoichi: I think infrastructure—like power, electricity, transport networks, and so on—are extremely important when thinking about efficiency. How do you view that?

Hiroshi: The complete liberalization of infrastructure would have been ideal, yet we ended up with a situation in which regulations are thoroughly enforced.

Ryoichi: No economic groups like Keidanren exist in the United States.

Hiroshi: In the United States, the Office of the United States Trade Representative (USTR) is fulfilling a role like the METI here.

Ryoichi: Right, but the USTR is an organization that dealt with external affairs, so it's different from METI.

Hiroshi: In Japan's case, the predecessor to METI, at the time called the Ministry of International Trade and Industry, was the government organization in charge of external trade, dealing with the crucial theme of how to best increase exports from Japan. I believe that Keidanren developed through its work on that theme.

Ryoichi: It's a fact that Japanese corporations are protected by the government in several ways. In Europe, too, I think we have seen the creation of a system of protection since the time of the European Communities. My basic belief is that if it is true that Japan lost its productivity because of protective policies, then I don't think we have an option to recover from that. In terms of competing in the international arena without the protection of the government, there isn't a metric by which to measure the strength of competitiveness, but I suppose productivity per capita might be a good index.

Hiroshi: Looking at the data, Japan's productivity is very low.

Ryoichi: I wish that journalists and economists and other such intellectuals would do more to drive home that point. In the United States, many think that it's a bad thing for the government to protect industry like we do in Japan. Free competition is fundamental. The U.S. mind-set is that if negative elements emerge from free competition, we should correct them as they emerge. Of course, in the United States they also have the promotion of IT as a national policy, but I think the fundamental thought is that it is bad to protect industry.

Hiroshi: I have doubts about whether bureaucrats or politicians have the vision needed to select which technologies and services are going to catalyze the growth of each industry in the future.

Ryoichi: It's hard to foster the kind of vision among bureaucrats and politicians that will allow them to see the age they live in.

Hiroshi: I created a prescription to cure the Japanese disease that you mentioned. But the main points and important proposals about fundamentally changing the nature of the Japanese economy were consistently put off or postponed as topics of debate. And conversely, I feel like the scenarios developed by the government bureaucracy always made it on the agenda.

Ryoichi: What sorts of scenarios were proposed by the bureaucracy?

Hiroshi: The simplest example to explain the situation would be the restart of nuclear power stations. No matter how many times we tried to say that we should move forward—with caution—on that issue, they would not hear it. I asked at the end for them to at least consider both sides of the issue, but they were absolutely against it. There weren't many things proposed by the private-sector members that made it into the growth strategy, but many of the proposals from METI made it in.

Ryoichi: I would never know it just by reading the newspaper articles.

Hiroshi: When the U.S. economy was performing poorly in the 1980s, there was a time when a group of mostly business leaders got together and submitted a proposal to the U.S. government. And the government received that proposal and considered the creation of policies. But here, this time, METI started with a draft of the growth strategy from the very beginning. It's not a nice way of putting it, but I felt that a lot of things happened in the Industrial Competitiveness Council that were fueled by politics—by a desire for excuses to oppose the will of the prime minister. Proposals from the private sector that did make it into the growth strategy were things that did not interfere with the scenarios created by METI, the Ministry of Finance, and other bureaucrats.

Now, I would not say that the Industrial Competitiveness Council was entirely pointless. We managed to include a recommendation to participate in treaty negotiations for the Trans-Pacific Partnership, and to an extent, some of the assertions of the private-sector members were accepted in the Abe administration growth strategy, including those related to the sale of over-the-counter or nonprescription drugs over the Internet.

That said, I do not think enough was done to recommend a major shift, such as regulatory reform, or to create any new frameworks. We were also not able to include enough on the biggest problems related to competitiveness, such as corporate governance issues. There is still much to do. I believe that having passed the House of Councillors election in July 2013, we are entering a critical phase in which it will be possible for the Abe administration to promote economic reconstruction in the truest sense, including in relation to issues such as changes to governance systems and reforms in the agriculture and medical industries.

Abenomics should be commended in many ways, but I'm disappointed that we could not do away with the ideas of state capitalism that are entrenched within it. These plans call for massive investments in fields specially selected by government officials. Bureaucracy-led state capitalism [moratorium policies] is dangerous. I wanted to write this book so that we could bring these issues to the public.

The Nature of Innovation

Hiroshi: Among the five factors that I proposed, I want to first explain innovation. Where does innovation happen? One place it happens is in the academic world, in universities and research institutions. The second place is in major corporations, and the third is in venture or start-up firms. What is important here is to separate invention and innovation. They are not the same thing. For example, isn't the invention of the Apple iPhone really just a combination of technology that already existed?

Ryoichi: Well, they didn't use such revolutionary technology in terms of the device itself, but the combination of applications, the user interface, and the design was revolutionary.

Hiroshi: This is your area of specialty, so I realize that I am preaching to the choir here, but I believe that innovation is the main driver of economic growth. This is a theory of Joseph Schumpeter. He clearly stated that inventions and innovation were two different things. I think we need to really think about that. It seems to me that the politicians, bureaucrats, and economists of Japan are mixing up these two concepts.

Schumpeter was one of the 20th century's major economists. He said that innovation was the product of new combinations, and he proposed five patterns of innovation:

1. The production of a new good
2. The introduction of a new method of production
3. The development of a new market
4. The acquisition of a new source of supply of raw materials
5. The emergence of a new organization of any industry

I believe that these patterns have all changed with the emergence of the Internet. If we stick to the principle of face-to-face delivery in which you must meet with the other parties in a transaction to make decisions, or the principle of on-paper delivery in which the points decided on are always written down, it will be difficult to create new innovation. No matter if we are talking about education or health care or business-to-business services, new services will be created through the combination of new things in complex ways. And it is a problem that it is difficult to make that happen.

Another problem is that the technology and policies of Japan do not meet global standards. This is because they are being developed only within Japan. Some global companies are addressing this problem. For example, look at Samsung. They are working to create frameworks that can be developed into international standards. Every year, they send hundreds of employees to dozens of countries around the world. They have a system of regional specialists within the country, and they have the attitude that people should first go to a market and look around before doing anything else. They have their employees stay abroad for a year. While the employees are abroad, they are free to go to school or conduct research, or even in extreme cases, to do nothing. That is how Samsung is developing its globalization strategy.

Incidentally, Samsung is trying to do all of this with only South Korean employees. Our approach at Rakuten is completely different. At Rakuten we are not trying to have our Japanese employees lead the way. It might sound extreme, but I don't think there would be anything wrong if our management team was entirely foreign nationals.

The next thing that I think is important for the creation of innovation is the development of an environment in which it is easy to propose new solutions. This calls for policies that resolve work-related issues. In other words, eliminate regulations and create an environment in which it is possible to do the things that have not been possible up until now. If that was done, I think the basic pattern would be the creation of new markets followed by the emergence of new technology and development of new innovations. So the most important issue is how to eliminate regulations.

For example, even if distance education is possible using IT, education that is not carried out in a face-to-face setting is not awarded full academic credits. Mixed medical care service regulations that prevent the free selection of medical care services present another issue. The obstacles to innovation created by regulations are a big problem.

An important issue related to this is how to best increase the number of venture or start-up firms giving rise to innovation. Because venture firms are accountable to their investors, and because they face the threat that if they do not act fast, they may fail, they work with a greater sense of urgency than large corporations do.

Ryoichi: The word "venture" comes from "adventure."

Hiroshi: Right. Venture firms need to be adventurous. And what's more, our efforts to create innovation require us to bring more foreign nationals into Japan. The reason Rakuten is growing at such a fast pace is because we are hiring foreign engineers.

Ryoichi: From which countries do you hire the most people?

Hiroshi: We have some people from the United States, but most are from Northern and Eastern Europe. I notice a lot of people with Japanese wives. [laughs] Incidentally, this isn't just happening at Rakuten—Andy Rubin, who developed the Android operating system used in mobile phones, is also married to a Japanese woman, as is Jerry Yang, the cofounder of Yahoo!

Ryoichi: They're married to Japanese people? People in Sweden, Norway, and other Northern European countries also seem to like Japanese people.

Hiroshi: They are getting inspiration from Japan through their wives.

Ryoichi: They complement each other. There is inspiration to be found in Japan, but not that many people can turn that inspiration into a business.

Schumpeter's Contribution

Hiroshi: Since we have been talking about innovation, could you tell me more about Schumpeter's economy theory?

Ryoichi: A former professor of mine, Kobe University's Hiroshi Shinjo, studied abroad in Germany just before World War I, when Joseph Schumpeter was working as a professor at Bonn University. He was an economist who was known to be a genius at a young age, and he used to serve as the finance minister of Austria. Among the Japanese students who learned directly from Dr. Schumpeter were former professor at Tokyo University Seiichi Tobata and former president of Hitotsubashi University Ichiro Nakayama. Schumpeter moved to Harvard University after that, but when he did so he took the Trans-Siberian Railway across China and even visited his pupils in Japan at Kobe University of Commerce [currently Kobe University] and the Tokyo College of Commerce [currently Hitotsubashi University].

Schumpeter was originally from a high-class family and was a man of extreme pride. At Harvard he fell in love with an American woman and got married, and I hear that he became quite Americanized. His most famous theory was the one that you described a moment ago about innovation. Schumpeter was a man who wondered why the economy could develop the way it does considering that if we take price competition to the extreme, we should see the complete extermination of profit. When an economy expands, the number of workers increases, and the amount of wages that needs to be paid out increases as well. Real expansion is not just about an increase in scale; it is actually about a continued rise in productivity through innovation. Schumpeter thought that this rise in productivity was the true marker of economic growth.

I believe that the contribution of Schumpeter to economics was extremely large. Up until that point, economics focused on the study of equilibrium and things like average rates of profit, as represented by the ideas of the English economist Alfred Marshall. It was thought that profit was being used for capital or for investments into research and development. Schumpeter believed differently, that innovation itself was the source of profit. That was his most important academic point.

I believe that we see only a handful of economists as remarkable as Schumpeter every hundred years, but it wasn't just his ideas that were remarkable. It is also amazing how many of his pupils became excellent economists. Schumpeter was involved with many topics, but he did not force his theory on his disciples. I think even Schumpeter himself understood after World War II that economic ideas like his were not applicable as the times changed, and that the study of economics needed to change as well. And so he let his students study what they wanted to. For that, too, I respect Schumpeter very much.

Dozens of his students became renowned economists. Among them was Paul Sweezy, a Keynesian economist [believing in the work of John Maynard Keynes, who postulated that governments should create jobs through active fiscal stimulus in order to overcome unemployment and recessions], who was at the same time also well versed in Marxian economics. He was apparently also rich, and so he did not look for work at any single university but instead came and went from different places as a visiting professor.

Back then, I was also interested in socialism, and I often talked with Sweezy.

Schumpeter passed away in 1950, but if he had lived just about 10 years longer, I would have been able to meet him in person at Harvard.

Hiroshi: I think the idea that price competition could lead to the end of profit is very interesting.

Ryoichi: Yes, that was something Schumpeter thought about extensively. According to the empiricism promoted in the United Kingdom, statistics suggested that the average rate of profit should be 20 percent. Schumpeter believed that as competition continued, the excess rate of profit would disappear. His ideas on innovation were the result of that thought and the desire to pursue an answer to that contradiction between theory and reality.

Hiroshi: Even today, METI seems to think that average profits should be protected, which is an idea so antiquated it goes back to even before Schumpeter. [laughs] There are certain aspects of French winemaking, such as the soil where the wine is cultivated or the traditional techniques used, that cannot really be copied by other countries, but in Japan, we are seeing the breakdown of the concept that Japanese-made products are special. Put another way, we are seeing the end of excess profit. I think that is the essence of branding. Then again, I don't suppose that Schumpeter had much to say about the concept of brands.

Ryoichi: The term *brand* was coined by Schumpeter's student James Duesenberry. For example, why is it that the famous French brand Louis Vuitton can be so profitable? Because it differentiates its products. Duesenberry's contribution was to state this principle in what he called the demonstration effect.

Hiroshi: You don't mean the same Duesenberry whose home I once lived in for about a month? [laughs] He was a great man.

Ryoichi: He was a very good person and was close to everyone in our family. He visited Japan three times or so. He was a big boss in the field of economics, and I mean that with great affection. He wrote his theory on the demonstration effect in 1949, right after the end of World War II, and it propelled him to instant fame.

Hiroshi: The brand effect is not something that works geometrically. People will buy Sony products if they trust that brand and think that they make good products. But internationally, we are seeing the breakdown of the Sony brand. It occurs to me that innovation is fairly important for the creation of a brand.

Ryoichi: Just after the end of World War II, there was a conflict in the field of economics called the consumption-function controversy, which related to consumption propensity. Consumption propensity means the ratio of income that people are willing to spend on consumption. The demonstration effect emerged as a part of the conversation about which elements contributed to the way consumption propensity was decided. There was the thought that when people buy products, they do not just think about whether the product is good or bad, but they also consider the demonstration effect. And that demonstration effect is corroborated by shifts in macroeconomic statistics related to the total share of consumption within aggregate amounts of income. This is why Duesenberry became so famous so quickly at such a young age.

Hiroshi: And I stayed in his house as a student without knowing anything about it! [laughs]

Building Infrastructure

Hiroshi: From the perspective of prioritizing innovation, I wonder if Schumpeter didn't take a cool stance to the fiscal policy of monetarists and Keynesians?

Ryoichi: No, from what I have heard, Schumpeter thought a lot about the Keynesian framework. Then again, Keynes was the top economist at the renowned British university Cambridge. Schumpeter may have harbored some feelings of envy toward him.

Hiroshi: One of the three arrows of Abenomics is the use of Keynesian fiscal stimuli. However, because the multiplier effect of fiscal stimuli is low, I suppose the government will need to build a lot of expressways and bridges.

Ryoichi: When you say the multiplier effect, you are referring to times when investment increases and the resulting increase in income is greater than the increased investment amount? For example, a fiscal stimulus of 100 million yen will yield an increase in gross domestic product or national income several times larger than the initial investment. That amplification is the multiplier effect. If the government invests 10 billion yen, then the public will consume that funding as income and use that income for consumption again. The amount of money circulating through the economy will gradually decrease, but adding everything together, the effect on national income should total around 40 billion yen. Usually the multiplier effect should quadruple the initial investment, although in reality it usually approximately doubles it. The remaining money goes somewhere else.

One explanation for that is fiscal leakage. It is extremely important to have as little leakage as possible and to figure out ways to increase the number of times that the consumption and investment cycle occurs. If you can do so, you can enhance the effect of your initial 10-billion-yen investment just by changing systems. That point is something that people in charge of policy at the Ministry of Finance, the Policy Board of the Bank of Japan, and economists must always think about. It does not cost anything to change a system, and doing so can enhance the multiplier effect. I think this is an important point.

Hiroshi: In terms of the multiplier effect, as you explained, the public consumes, and that consumption becomes income. That is the multiplier effect you are talking about, right? But there is also another kind of multiplier effect that refers to the creation of new markets and enhancement of the economy's efficiency through investments in communications infrastructure and education. I think those two ideas get mixed up.

Ryoichi: With the term *investment* as well; there is both demand-side investment and supply-side investment. When talking about the multiplier effect, attention up to this point has tended to focus on the demand side, but the multiplier effect caused by infrastructure investments on the supply side is important, too.

Hiroshi: I feel like the bureaucrats of the Ministry of Finance think about only the demand-side multiplier effect.

Ryoichi: It's a terrible thing. If we were seeing a situation like in the 1930s when unemployment was high, it would be fine to think about only the demand side, but that isn't the situation in Japan.

Hiroshi: In a prosperous society like Japan, I wonder if the multiplier effect on consumption won't really increase that much, even if we do increase income. By which I mean that I wonder if we haven't reached a point in which the effect of fiscal stimuli is not as great as it once was?

For that reason, I think there is a need to put precedence on thoroughly computing the supply-side multiplier effect over work on the multiplier effect usually talked about in economics textbooks.

Ryoichi: Yes. In the past, we have seen palliative economic stimuli, but the current situation is different.

Hiroshi: Because even if there is a multiplier effect, that effect will gradually decrease, and I think that at some point we will even see a negative economic effect due to leakages.

Ryoichi: That is why the design of systems is so important.

Hiroshi: I believe that the greatest multiplier effect comes from communications infrastructure. And in that case, I wonder if there isn't a need for a drastic measure in which we might thoroughly invest in communications infrastructure, nationalize it, and make it free. That is what I proposed when I thought up the IT autobahn concept that I touched on earlier. Based on the concept of the German autobahn, this idea calls for the nationalization of IT infrastructure and the creation of the world's most advanced, free, and open communications environment. I think this would be revolutionary. Investment in education is another issue. I don't think that investment needs only to go toward hard infrastructure. What do you think of that?

Ryoichi: Japan doesn't have abundant natural resources. Our people are everything. I actually think it is more important for us to invest in people, although I doubt whether this opinion is shared widely in this country.

Hiroshi: For example, the return on investment (ROI) for investments into education—in other words, the amount of expenditure in comparison to the effect produced—is actually more than 20 percent. It is in fact far higher than the ROI of any other infrastructure investment.

Turkey, which competed with Tokyo in the bid to host the 2020 Summer Olympics, is making an annual investment of 100 billion yen into English-language education in order to improve the English-language ability of the population there. You may think that 100 billion yen is a lot of money, but the budget for reconstruction following the Great East Japan Earthquake is 25 trillion yen. It is a mere 1/250th of that amount.

Ryoichi: The need for English-language education has been talked about for some time, but we still have not achieved our goals related to that. At the end of the day, we may not be able to do this without education reform.

How should the money gained from innovation be used? Some part of it will go toward labor costs. We must change the tax system if we are going to get rid of economic disparity. But it would be a terrible thing if the tax system set up in an effort to reduce disparity also stifled innovation.

Hiroshi: In the beginning, the economy of the Soviet Union did really well. Their planned economy worked. But at some point, people started to feel that working no longer had meaning, and the economy slowed down.

Ryoichi: A precondition for the development of an economy is surely the stable maintenance of economic order. And so I think the debate inevitably ends up being about the extent to which people who make money should give back to society and the extent to which they should use their money for innovation.

Hiroshi: Whether we are talking about socialism or the kind of organizational system seen in Japan, there are always free riders who work without taking risks. Or rather, a special class of society is extremely inefficient. But in principle, as the Japanese expression goes, "Those who don't work should not eat." I don't think there is anything positive we can say about people who make money off disparities in the financial system rather than making investments based on a long-term vision. That is why I always say that morality is even more important than legality.

Business Innovation

Hiroshi: Schumpeter believed that innovation was the source of economic growth, assuming appropriate fiscal and monetary policies are in place. And the reason for that is related to what you explained earlier—excess profit decreases with time.

In the end, innovation does not need to mean inventions like induced pluripotent stem cells or anything else. The emergence of new discoveries is absolutely a good thing, but even without inventions, a country can still come out ahead of other countries through global expansion and market capabilities [explained in Chapter 5] and through its business innovation capabilities.

Again, look at Samsung: They have not created any new technologies or products. In fact, Japan is where the inventions have been happening, such as the development of DVDs and CDs or the invention of fiber-optic cable. It is important to have technological capabilities, but I feel it is more important to have business innovation capabilities that can make the combination of new things possible. Even the iPhone is just a piece of technology combining a mobile phone, the Internet, and a camera. As an idea, it is exactly the same as i-mode,[2] yet the iPhone went global and i-mode went Galapagos. All of this is why we need to

---

[2]i-mode was the world's first web service for a feature phone, developed by NTT DoCoMo in 1999, which was adopted only by Japanese cellphones and compatible only in Japan.

take a step forward in international competition and develop the capability to expand business globally.

At one time, Sony had this capability. How did it lose that? I believe that the reason is simple—the founder of Sony, Akio Morita, passed away. Similarly, Steve Jobs passed away, and Apple's innovation has stagnated. Google is a slightly different case. They have a framework in place that enables innovation. In the end, I think management capabilities are extremely important for business innovation. Business leaders without the ability to analyze global trends or those lacking global expansion capabilities should excuse themselves from positions of power on principle. Or if not, companies without these kinds of leaders should be absorbed by companies that do have such leaders.

Ryoichi: If you were the CEO of Sony, how would you reform it?

Hiroshi: That is something that I could not know unless I actually tried it. [laughs] But if I were CEO of Sony, I think I would be able to do something with it. Rakuten acquired Sony's prepaid e-money service Edy to start Rakuten Edy. Under Sony, Edy was in the red from the very beginning, but we have made it profitable since bringing it into the Rakuten group.

Related to that, I would have you know that the rate at which people open new businesses in Japan is as low as 4 percent. Actually, the rate of business failure is also 4 percent. One reason for that is the moratorium policy of national and local governments. A typical example of these kinds of policies is the relief measures for small- and medium-sized enterprises (SMEs) being implemented by the Tokyo Metropolitan Government (TMG). TMG invested 100 billion yen in 2004 to create ShinGinko Tokyo, Limited, in order to support SMEs facing harsh business conditions through the provision of unsecured loans and other measures. In just three years, the bank was nearly 100 billion yen in debt, and it took on an additional public investment of 40 billion yen. These policies implement moratoriums so that failing companies do not fail. It's stupid. Bad companies should fail; it is good for the world. Because people are indomitable—even if they fail once, they go on to produce something new.

Ryoichi: Because that failure gives birth to wisdom and invention. It gives rise to innovation.

Hiroshi: The relief measures given to Japan Airlines (JAL) are the definition of a moratorium policy. I have many friends at JAL in my personal life, but I think it would have been for the best if the company had been allowed to fail. If it had, we would have seen the emergence in Japan of low-cost carriers, and plane ticket prices would have fallen. And that would stir demand for the travel business, as well as businesses in areas outside of major cities. It would have been a good thing. But instead, a massive national investment was made, and we lost that opportunity.

Ryoichi: Schumpeter had a famous phrase describing that: *creative destruction*. If you mean to create, you cannot avoid destruction.

Hiroshi: The point is that we should gradually transfer goods and services that have lost their added value or that have low added value to companies overseas. At the same time, within Japan we should foster excellent human resources who can initiate innovation, and we should draw them from abroad as well.

Ryoichi: On that point, China may not be gathering people from abroad. No matter how much an American likes China, most stay only for a short period. I don't think there are very many people who move to the

Shanghai area for a long period, settle down, and establish a business.

Hiroshi: Right. But at the same time, China has created a framework at the national level by which it is sending its human resources to Stanford and MIT and then bringing them back home. Samsung is doing the same thing. I think it would be a huge mistake to think that China [or Samsung] can only imitate what others are doing, as has been the case in the past. The people who gain PhDs from America's top universities return home like salmon. [laughs]

Ryoichi: How should Japan interact with China?

Hiroshi: I would propose that an appropriate distance be maintained and that we treat each other like adults. And I think we must deepen our friendly relationships with neighboring countries and the United States. As you have often said, it is extremely important to advance friendly relations with South Korea.

Ryoichi: Absolutely. We cannot overlook the value of South Korea for Japan–China relations.

Hiroshi: In the past, Japan was number one in terms of both technology and intellectual property, but since the emergence of the Internet, the gap between countries has narrowed. And I think our 100 million to China's 1 billion population difference has been very effective for that. India faces many religious and class issues, but China does not. And because it has a kind of controlled economy, it can quickly advance infrastructure development.

Ryoichi: I am extremely interested to see what will happen in China from now on.

Hiroshi: I think we will see the emergence of new innovation to an extent, but I doubt that China will outdo us. Japan not only has more diversity than China, but we also possess a level of tolerance that enables us to accept many different cultures. I think we can differentiate ourselves with that, and I think people believe that Japan is a good country.

Summary

- What is economic growth? It is the continuous development of innovations arising from combinations of new connections. Eliminate the principles of face-to-face and on-paper delivery, and construct an environment in which innovation can occur.
- The role and purpose of the government should extend no further than the creation of platforms for industry. Advance thorough regulatory reform.
- Set the key KPIs needed to change the entire economic structure of Japan.
- Promote the IT autobahn concept to construct a faster and cheaper communications infrastructure throughout the world.

2 | The Power to Operate

Workforce Fluidity

Hiroshi: I would like to discuss the power to operate. There is this impression that Japan's power to operate is extremely high—after all, everyone knows about Toyota's high levels of productivity.

Ryoichi: The power to operate—would that be the operational capacity needed to realize innovation?

Hiroshi: You can call it operational capacity or productivity, but either way, looking at the overall statistics, Japan is actually extremely inefficient. Looking at data from the International Labour Organization, Japan's gross domestic product (GDP) per worker is U.S. $44,500. This puts Japan at 23rd in the world. It is clear that Japan is extremely inefficient. The reality is pretty shocking and very different from what the general population assumes to be true.

What's more, this figure was from 2011. Accounting for the weak yen and the current yen–dollar exchange rate, Japan's GDP per worker drops even further. I estimate that number is now probably less than U.S. $40,000. On top of that, the size of Japan's workforce is actually shrinking. I believe we are facing a very grave situation. Japan's power to operate is so low because of the underutilization of IT and the excessive costs of the public sector. [I will examine these two issues in more detail in Chapter 4.]

Going back to Japanese employment, I think we have to address the lack of balance. On the one hand, you have insufficient workers in sectors such as nursing care and agriculture, and, on the other hand, you have many sectors with very low labor participation rates. Overall, the distribution of the workforce is suboptimal.

Another issue is employment rigidity. The lifetime employment system is producing negative effects and is restricting the development of a fluid workforce for companies and universities. As a result, middle-aged workers remain at their companies in perpetuity, while employment opportunities for the young are disappearing.

Japanese companies are responsible for the current state of affairs, and the biggest reason behind these developments is the inadequacy of their managers. If Japanese companies were to appoint the best people available—people who have accumulated a variety of experiences on the global stage—then they would be able to raise their competitiveness. In reality, however, under the lifetime employment system, homegrown employees are promoted to managerial positions based on age rather than skill or global experience.

In addition, because of the rigidity of the labor market, companies are unable to dismiss employees.

In my opinion, it makes more sense to promote workforce fluidity and develop a structure whereby workers can move into more productive jobs. In Japan, once you hire employees, you cannot then let them go. This results in a negative cycle where, to put it crassly, "workers don't get hired because they can't get fired." This is one reason why no one wants to hire more workers even when the economy is doing better.

The easing of employment regulations was originally meant to be included in the Abe administration's growth strategy. But in the end it was left out, probably because of fears over negative public reaction in an election year.

One issue associated with the topic of building a secure workforce is the hiring of more women. Hiring more women is absolutely essential, but there are limits to what this measure can achieve on its own. This being the case, we have to consider the active introduction of foreign workers and immigration-related matters.

Ryoichi: I agree, for the most part, but I would advise recognizing that differences among countries exist when it comes to employment-termination regulations. There are significant differences between the United States, the countries of the European Union, and Japan. In the United States, employment regulations are relatively loose, and it is quite easy for a company to temporarily lay off workers when it is performing badly or for a variety of other reasons. The European Union has proposed a flexible employment system among all member countries. Japan, however, has some of the strictest employment-termination regulations among countries in the Organization for Economic Co-operation and Development (OECD).

During Japan's rapid growth period, these regulations made sense from the perspective that the best way to raise productivity was for companies to maintain and educate their workforce. However, now that we are not faced with rapid growth, it no longer makes sense to hold onto a workforce that is incurring huge costs. For this reason, it is extremely important to ensure workforce fluidity, both among large corporations and between large companies and small- and medium-sized enterprises. In order to develop new industries, we have to move the factors of production, and at the end of the day, without the movement of workers, industries themselves will not change.

Hiroshi: One of the problems with the Japanese labor market is that the workforce is thought of as a uniform entity. In the United States, white-collar workers receive preferential treatment in the form of white-collar exemptions, whereas in Japan, white-collar and blue-collar workers are treated the same way.

I am chairman of the board of the Tokyo Philharmonic Orchestra, and the members of the orchestra also belong to a lifetime employment system. Once orchestra members are hired, they can perform for the rest of their lives, from their early twenties through retirement. There was actually a case where the New National Theatre, in Tokyo, was taken to court over the dismissal of a member of its choir. Regardless of whether you are a skilled performer or not, members of choirs and orchestras are employed for life. The Tokyo Philharmonic Orchestra does exercise self-discipline, and if it decides that one of the members is not very good, then that person is unable to perform with the orchestra, but the issue regarding employment remains.

Ryoichi: Performance is bound to suffer under the lifetime employment system.

Hiroshi: The bigger problem is that talented young performers can't get into any of these orchestras or theaters.

Out of all the fresh graduates from music and performing arts colleges, probably no more than four or five manage to get into one of the top Japanese orchestras.

Ryoichi: Wow, that's nothing.

Hiroshi: The Seoul Philharmonic Orchestra in South Korea, on the other hand, changed its structure. By allowing young musicians into the orchestra, it managed to vault up the orchestral rankings. Frankly speaking, younger musicians are probably better than senior musicians, in part because, unlike in the past, effective practice methods are now well established. This is a good example of why the employment of professionals needs to be liberalized.

Ryoichi: I think so, too. Universities are professional groups of researchers, and yet academic organizations are the most rigid.

Hiroshi: I doubt it is easy to dismiss university employees, either.

Ryoichi: In some cases in the United States, a term-based system has been introduced, but for the most part, university employees cannot be dismissed.

Privatization

Hiroshi: Going back to the beginning of the discussion, I think companies that are no longer productive should go out of business. Venture or start-up firms are at the opposite end of the scale: They are hiring. They then absorb the flow of workers that have been freed up.

Ryoichi: That is the way it should be.

Hiroshi: In Japan, despite the superior levels of productivity in factories, looking at the overall statistics, Japan's productivity is rather poor. The reason for this is the high expenses incurred by headquarters in terms of personnel costs and administrative costs.

Ryoichi: I agree.

Hiroshi: While on a recent visit to Harvard Business School, I attended a lecture on whether Japan would become the next Greece. The public sector is far too big in Greece, and I think anything that can be handled by the private sector should be privatized.

In Japan's case, the cabinet under former Prime Minister Junichiro Koizumi promoted privatization and the streamlining of the central government. However, under subsequent administrations, particularly while the Democratic Party of Japan (DPJ)[1] was in power, we have once again seen the burgeoning of the central government.

The public sector should basically be privatized, with public-sector employees joining private companies. In addition to that, the current extremely rigid employment-termination regulations in the public sector should be liberalized. This should result in a growth in hiring. As things stand, young people cannot find jobs, because it is impossible to dismiss anyone. In my opinion, it does not make sense to protect middle-aged workers and neglect younger ones.

Some have pointed out that it is difficult for middle-aged workers to change jobs midcareer, but at the same time, there are insufficient workers in the service industry and in the nursing care field. They might have to take a pay cut, but I believe there is plenty of opportunity for middle-aged workers to find new jobs or to start a new venture firm. With universities, I imagine most

---

[1] The DPJ, founded in 1998, is known as a centrist to center-left political party in Japan. The DPJ defeated the long-dominant Liberal Democratic Party in the 2009 election and was the ruling party until 2012.

employees tend to stay at the same institution until they retire. What is the situation like there?

Ryoichi: At universities some professors are employed for life despite never writing a single academic paper, and ultimately output comes down to each individual's conscience and their abilities. Furthermore, professors have to fulfill educational responsibilities and teach students as well, so to some extent they are forgiven for not conducting the most creative research. However, some universities face a dilemma where the university is run solely by people who do not carry out any research but do take an interest in university administration, while the most talented researchers are busy performing creative research and have zero interest in the administration of the university. In the United States, it is common for talented members of the university on the academic side to also take an interest in important administrative decisions.

Hiroshi: Ultimately, I think it is important to appoint the right person to the right job. Even at Rakuten, plenty of our employees leave the company to work elsewhere. All positions have their limitations; so if people are not satisfied with their jobs, it makes complete sense to quit Rakuten and join another company or to start one of their own.

At Samsung, they are satisfied with only retaining 50 percent of new hires 10 years down the line. So if Samsung hires 100 new employees, they are satisfied if 50 of these employees are still with Samsung in 10 years' time, which makes the yearly employee turnover rate about 5 percent. So from a management perspective, Samsung is doing a great job. Management of Japanese companies is much poorer. Even in Germany, it may look like the workforce is not very fluid, but in reality the existence of a white-collar exemption is helping to

promote workforce fluidity. In addition, companies that
are designated as professional firms, such as law firms,
accounting firms, and consultancies, have almost total
freedom when it comes to employment-termination
decisions.

Ryoichi: Could you explain what a white-collar
exemption is?

Hiroshi: It is a system where instead of providing
white-collar workers with an executive allowance, they
are made exempt from a variety of regulations, including
working hours. Exempt workers' wages are determined
under an annual salary system with a legal limit on how
much salaries can be cut by.

Ryoichi: I see.

Hiroshi: The introduction of a white-collar exemption in
Japan has actually been discussed. In 2007 the Ministry of
Health, Labour and Welfare submitted a bill on the
matter, where exemptions would apply to workers
receiving a minimum of 9 million yen annually, and who
are engaged in five specific types of work, including
planning, research, and investigation. Currently,
discussions are ongoing regarding whether to bring the
minimum applicable annual salary down to 7 million yen,
or even 4 million yen.

Ryoichi: I see.

Hiroshi: The problem for Japan right now is the lack of
workers in growth fields. For example, I mentioned
previously that the field of inexpensive air travel and
low-cost carriers (LCCs) is growing at a tremendous rate,
but because the government bailed out JAL, there is a
labor shortage in the field. JAL should have been allowed
to go bankrupt and the massive workforce that would
then be freed up should have entered the more
innovatively managed LCC sector.

Ryoichi: I see. So you believe that labor should have flowed into new airline companies?

Hiroshi: Foreigners and JAL retirees have gone on to work for LCCs. Operations are simply efficient, and wages should be satisfactory.

Ryoichi: I see.

Hiroshi: In terms of job turnover, from a management perspective, I believe it is best to maintain an appropriate rate. At Rakuten as well, we believe it is necessary to maintain a certain level of turnover. At the same time, though, too high a turnover rate is not good for the management of the company.

Still, 3 percent just does not achieve enough turnover. This might be fine for Rakuten, which is still growing, but to some degree a mature company has to cull people or promote automation in order to raise productivity.

Lifetime Employment

Ryoichi: In the end, a company is only as good as its employees. Employment is the most important factor for companies to consider when they are looking to grow. Technology is important, too, but employees develop technology and create products.

Until now, the lifetime employment system was accepted as the standard in Japan. Companies trained and developed human resources internally, and by internalizing this process, the knowledge and technical capabilities of the company's entire workforce were raised. However, now that the lifetime employment system has broken down, we are likely to see major changes in the ways employees are used.

Hiroshi: For example, if you include all of the employees from the merchants and facilities registered to Rakuten Ichiba and Rakuten Travel, Rakuten has in some way contributed to around 300,000 jobs domestically, which is 30 times more than the number of actual Rakuten employees. As you can see, the creation of new venture or start-up firms also generates new jobs. However, even though Japan's economy needs to transition to one that produces more high-value-added goods, much of the workforce is currently concentrated in low-value-added work. On top of that, various mechanisms in Japanese society maintain these conditions, so hardly any companies are going out of business. As a result, Japan has fallen into a negative spiral of declining competitiveness.

Ryoichi: In economics, Japan's industrial composition is seen as being divided into three components, namely (1) primary industries, which include agriculture and other similar industries; (2) secondary industries, which are manufacturing and the like; and (3) tertiary industries, which are service-related industries. Nowadays, though, Japan's industrial composition has largely changed. Even the companies that make up the Keidanren are now primarily manufacturing companies. So, in that sense, the mechanisms in Japanese society have changed.

Hiroshi: The manufacturing industry is very influential. Originally the Keidanren was an organization with companies like Tokyo Electric Power Company at the core, and then associated companies formed around these core companies. Among these groups there were two types of manufacturing companies: those that were deeply entwined in Japan's industrial structure and those that were trying to compete globally.

When average students graduate at age 22, in the brief time they spend finding their first job, they are extremely unlikely to hit the jackpot. In other words, they are extremely unlikely to join a company that is headed toward exponential growth in the future. [laughs] Despite this situation, once people join their first company, they are expected to work there for life. I find that bizarre. On the other side of things, in an age of workforce fluidity, I think it is frankly cruel to force companies to retain anyone they hire until that person retires. This is why irregular employment exists in Japan.

At Rakuten, it is completely normal for employees who have worked with us for 10 to 15 years to either continue working at Rakuten if they are doing a great job and getting paid well, or if that is not the case, to find work elsewhere. Samsung shares the same fundamental line of thinking on the matter. In sum, instead of taking a micro-level approach and sustaining employment at the company level, I think we need to take a macro-level approach and optimize the labor market. I also believe that fostering economic growth on a macro level generates capacity for employment.

In Japan, although it is not possible to terminate employment without a good reason, it is possible to terminate employment through voluntary early retirement, although in reality, the voluntary part is more like being pressured to quit.

Ryoichi: In Luxembourg not even voluntary early retirement is permissible, so in that regard, you could say things are still better in Japan.

Hiroshi: I believe it is possible to realize workforce fluidity in Japan, but taking the time to carefully explain the issue and gain understanding for it will be important. I think the first step should be the introduction of a white-collar exemption. Right now, we are seeing a kind of corporate socialism rather than state capitalism in Japan [laughs], and no turnover is taking place. I think, ultimately, the problem extends all the way to corporate governance. Japanese companies have fixed internal steps for promotion, so that even people with no managerial abilities make it to the top. As a result, Japan finds itself in a negative spiral of declining competitiveness. As I have mentioned time and again, Carlos Ghosn revived Nissan, and the return of Steve Jobs did the same for Apple. I believe the abolishment of the lifetime employment system is essential for Japan to regain its competitiveness.

Escaping Lifetime Employment

Ryoichi: Does Rakuten practice lifetime employment?

Hiroshi: Lifetime employment implies employing people from the day they enter the company to the time they reach retirement, but there is no actual legal definition. Rakuten does not practice lifetime employment, nor do we make severance payments.

Ryoichi: Does Rakuten have a mandatory retirement age?

Hiroshi: The mandatory retirement age is nothing more than a legally enforced age. Under the mandatory-retirement-age system, once workers reach a certain age, their employment is automatically terminated; however, according to the Law Concerning Stabilization of Employment of Older Persons, that age cannot be set below 60. The formulation of other measures is seen as necessary to ensure stable employment until the age of 65, such as the introduction of a continuous employment system. The term *mandatory retirement age* in itself is quite discriminatory, and chances are that using it in the United States would result in a lawsuit.

Ryoichi: In the United States, when employing people, it is illegal to even ask them their age.

Hiroshi: Right, so when you are looking at their job application, the best you can do is guess, "Okay, he graduated university in 1988, so he is probably around 48." Regardless, for Japan to recapture its economic dynamism, it absolutely has to move away from an employment system that is based on a mandatory retirement age. To expand this subject, let me ask you this: What does the study of labor economics entail?

Ryoichi: It involves the study of various labor-related issues from an economic point of view. It has been established as a branch of economics in its own right in the United States as well.

Hiroshi: I feel there are some points of similarity with Marxist thought.

Ryoichi: According to the labor theory of value in Marxian economics, the value of a good is determined by the amount of human labor it involves. Nowadays there are probably very few academics who study the labor theory of value. The idea that value is a product of labor and is determined by the amount of labor expended is simply not discussed.

Hiroshi: Although there are some people, like Robert Alan Feldman, chief economist for Morgan Stanley MUFG, who believe that GDP is primarily determined by a country's workforce.

Ryoichi: The idea that the amount of labor determines the overall level of production, right? This idea involves dividing any increase in production into the three factors of labor, technology, and capital, and examining the contributions of each, but this is also rarely discussed. Therefore, I think it is safe to say that the labor theory of

value is almost never discussed these days, probably
because capitalism is doing okay.

Hiroshi: Whenever innovation occurs, it raises the
productivity of the workforce, and the economy grows.

I actually have a great story about productivity. A long
time ago, when I was still working in a bank, we were
developing this new system that was costing several
hundred billion yen [several billion U.S. dollars].
Theoretically, the development of this system was
supposed to help streamline operations, with the ensuing
workforce reduction leading to reduced costs. In the end,
however, because personnel could not be cut, even
though we had developed this system, the number of
employees was not reduced, with the cost of the system
now being added on top of everything else. [laughs] It
sounds farcical, but it is a true story. The fact that we had
developed this system served no purpose in and of itself.
So it is impossible to foster innovation and create new
fields of business without first creating workforce fluidity.

Ryoichi: Did the Industrial Bank of Japan have a labor
union?

Hiroshi: It did, but to be honest, it sure did not feel like it.
It felt like labor unions were just where HR staff got
transferred to. [laughs] Labor unions are out of touch with
the times.

Ryoichi: Labor unions are systematically incorporated into
large Japanese corporations and have come to represent
the interests of the companies they belong to. I actually
have a friend who was the chairman of the labor union at
his company and then went on to become the company
vice president.

Hiroshi: If Japanese corporations are aiming for continuous
employment of their employees, then I think they should

pursue that goal, but they then need to think about how to use part-time and temporary workers.

Ryoichi: Employment conditions need to be diversified.

Hiroshi: That was the DPJ government's policy, but Japanese society is trending in the opposite direction and trying to rigidify employment conditions. But with rigid employment conditions, I think it will not be possible to keep up with the economic dynamism of the world, and in the end, workers will be worse off.

Immigration Problems

Hiroshi: One issue that arises in discussions about employment is immigration. The way I see it, with the globalization of the world economy, national borders are no longer very relevant. Under such circumstances and given that various Japanese industries are facing labor shortages, I think it makes sense to try to fill this shortage with foreign workers.

Ryoichi: There have been countless cases of Japanese people emigrating abroad in the postwar period. Significant numbers have moved to Brazil, for example. However, it seems to have been quite difficult for foreigners immigrating to Japan.

Hiroshi: I believe visa issues have made it difficult for them to come to Japan, although Kobe has a pretty large Indian community, right?

Ryoichi: During World War II in India, there were Indians who were pro-British, and those who were pro-Asian, and those who were pro-Asian moved to Kobe. The Kobe Club for Kobe's international community has many Indian members. They speak fluent Japanese, and their children attend Japanese schools, although their nationality is still Indian. During the war, they settled in Japan as foreign traders. They were treated well after the war, too, receiving much land in Kobe and growing quite rich. In fact, many of the luxury condos around Kitano are owned by Indians.

Hiroshi: There were also plenty of Germans in Kobe before the war, right?

Ryoichi: The Germans in Kobe were originally taken prisoner and housed in Kobe during World War I. Because of this, foreign trade later took off in the area.

Hiroshi: When speaking about immigration-related issues, the first of three points I would like to note is how to deal with high-level white-collar workers and blue-collar workers.

I recently visited the National Institute of Health (NIH) in the United States, and the researchers there were from all over the world, coming from places like China, Japan, Vietnam, and Eastern Europe, just to name a few locations. I saw hardly any Caucasian Americans. Furthermore, the dean and other senior professors at Harvard Business School are Indian, South Korean, and Chinese, among other nationalities. Their English is no longer the fluent English of the past.

It is impossible for all Japan's high-level workers to be Japanese. There are plans to create a Japanese version of the NIH, but this goal is extremely difficult to achieve with Japanese researchers alone. We need to consider how to attract the best and brightest—the top-class intellectuals—to Japan.

Second, there is a critical shortage of workers in Japan, and the only options are to either send factories overseas or bring workers into Japan. In my opinion, the latter is obviously the better option.

   Third, even if we increase the number of blue-collar workers, their children and their grandchildren will likely have transitioned to becoming white-collar workers. Many foreign workers came to the United States and joined the workforce as laborers, but their children and grandchildren received a high level of education and transitioned to becoming high-level workers, and now they are the ones supporting growth in the United States. In fact, some of the top students at places like Harvard and MIT are Vietnamese or South Korean students whose fathers came to work in the United States as factory workers.

Ryoichi: The second and third generations have worked hard and done well.

Hiroshi: Of course, in addition to their intelligence, these people have a really hungry attitude and have worked exceptionally hard. I am sure that growing up with a mixture of cultural influences has also helped make them stronger people.

Why English Needs to Be a Common Language in Japan

Hiroshi: In my case, when thinking about issues related to immigration, rather than trying to come up with a rigid definition for immigration and immigrants, I also consider the acceptance of foreign workers.

   Just today, while I was running in the Rakuten gym, there happened to be a foreign employee running beside me. So I asked, "Where are you from?" and we struck up a conversation. It turns out that, for the longest time, he had been working at Google, but he decided to start working for Rakuten because he identified with the company's corporate philosophy. Rakuten is currently attracting workers from around the world.

Ryoichi: That is pretty amazing.

Hiroshi: I believe the nursing care field also cannot be successful without the employment of foreign workers. Japanese workers would simply require too much compensation for it to be feasible. If one person costs 300,000 yen per month, then if you employ two people that is already 600,000 yen. There is no way the average person could afford that.

Ryoichi: I seem to remember that at one point there was a lot of talk about inviting Indonesian workers to Japan. What happened in the end?

Hiroshi: The test for gaining eligibility to stay in Japan was just awful. It was full of impossible Japanese questions that not even a native Japanese speaker could solve.

Ryoichi: Oh, so there was a barrier to entry. Why would the government do that?

Hiroshi: I believe that diversity is important and that, right now, Japan might be facing a historical turning point as globalization takes a huge leap forward.

Ryoichi: I think so, too.

Hiroshi: In Rakuten's case, just over 10 percent of the employees in our Tokyo offices are foreign nationals. Back in 2010, this number was only 2.5 percent, so it has really risen rapidly. In engineering, in particular, recently around 70 percent of our new hires are foreigners. We hire fresh graduates year-round, and about 30 percent of the hires are foreigners. If you include Japanese workers who graduated from an overseas university or at least spent some time studying abroad, this number goes higher still.

Ryoichi: How do these workers rank in the world?

Hiroshi: The foreigners working at Rakuten that were hired as fresh graduates out of foreign universities are extremely talented. We have graduates from famous universities like Harvard, Yale, Stanford, Cambridge, Peking University, and the Indian Institute of Technology.

Ryoichi: What was their motivation for working at Rakuten?

Hiroshi: They wanted to work in Asia but were reluctant to work in China. Many of them were fans of Japan, who had taken a liking to Japan after visiting on holiday, or who originally had an interest in Japanese culture. Also, although they wanted to work in Asia, they chose Rakuten because they felt that they could only work in companies that used English.

Ryoichi: I see, so English is indeed a pretty important factor.

Hiroshi: The prospect of working for a Japanese company also has its attractiveness, but there are still many hurdles when hiring foreign workers. Among these, the biggest hurdle is the language barrier.

Ryoichi: Right. If you cannot communicate your thoughts, how can you work together?

Hiroshi: I am sure you are aware of this, but since 2010 we have tried to make English the official language at Rakuten. Even the management committee of Vissel Kobe,[2] which I own as part of the Crimson Group, is slowly being run in English. Kenichi [Hiroshi's elder brother] is in charge of teaching the players English.

Ryoichi: Kenichi is a great teacher.

Hiroshi: English is not the official language of the Tohoku Rakuten Golden Eagles, though. For them, I think it's still a little too soon. That said, Munenori Kawasaki, who used to play for the SoftBank Hawks and is now with the Toronto Blue Jays in the U.S. Major League Baseball (MLB),

---

[2]Vissel Kobe is a professional Japanese soccer club with its hometown at Kobe city in Hyogo prefecture.

worked hard on his English, and his hilarious interviews have made him a real fan favorite. Until now, Japanese players in the MLB have always had interpreters with them, but Kawasaki opted not to have one.

The fact that professional Japanese soccer players can all speak English decently was probably originally sparked by Hidetoshi Nakata, the former Japanese national team player who also played for Perugia, Roma, and Parma in Italy, among other teams. Not only did he speak English, but all of a sudden you have this Japanese player who can speak Italian as well, and I think that set a precedent for the future. In the same way, I hope that, inspired by Kawasaki, we will see a change among professional Japanese baseball players as well. In my opinion, Japanese athletes trying to make it overseas should no longer use interpreters.

Ryoichi: That would be great.

Hiroshi: We faced many difficulties in converting to English at Rakuten, but as a result of this process, not only did the type of job applicants we receive change, but we were also attracting applicants of an even higher level.

Ryoichi: I thought there was a good chance Rakuten's experiment would be successful. The Japanese feel like they can never make any mistakes when speaking English. They get too caught up in minor points like forgetting the "s" when using the third person, but really, if you are just trying to communicate your thoughts, then broken English will do. In that sense, I thought that it would not be long before we would see some form of "Rakuten English." [laughs]

Hiroshi: Nonnative English is often called *Globish*. That's a term coined by IBM executive Jean-Paul Nerriere. It is a combination of the words "global" and "English." When Yukihiro Matsumoto, who developed the Ruby programming language, gave a speech at Rakuten, he joked that "Rakuten does not need to make English the official language. Poor English will do just fine!"

Ryoichi: That is a bit much.

Hiroshi: Currently, employees only have to reach a certain TOEIC score, but we are moving toward measuring employees' actual communication skills.

Ryoichi: You are not there yet, but it sounds like you are making steady progress.

Hiroshi: Rakuten's Englishnization in and of itself is a radical strategy for proactively employing foreign workers. I think Singapore is so successful because English is one of the official languages.

Ryoichi: If it were still only Chinese, then Singapore would probably not have achieved its current growth.

Hiroshi: If Japan were to make English a second official language, then it could become a huge Singapore, and that I believe is what would make Japan a real economic powerhouse, leaving China and South Korea in the dust.

Ryoichi: Are any other Japanese companies trying to make English the official company language?

Hiroshi: Unfortunately, not very many are, probably because most of the managers cannot speak English themselves.

Ryoichi: That is a major problem. I used to visit Sweden, and for quite a while back, the level of English there has been high enough to be considered an official language. In Sweden's case, the use of English started to spread after the end of World War II, so people around 40 years old and the generations that followed them can speak English, while the previous generations can speak only Swedish. This was the result of a significant shift in Swedish education.

Hiroshi: In order to raise levels of production, market mechanisms have to function properly. Next, you have to promote the best managers with great managerial abilities to the tops of organizations, by promoting fluidity among professionals. Naturally, opportunities also exist for those within the organization who are fighting their way up the corporate ladder, but if the right talent is not available within the company, then you have to be able to recruit externally. You need some kind of concept similar to trading for great players in professional baseball.

Growing the Population

Hiroshi: In terms of productivity, a declining population is a real problem, and we have to find some way to recover the shortfall in population. Put simply, Japan has to pick one of the following: either raise its birth rate or bring in foreigners.

Ryoichi: There is a tendency in Japan that by promoting women's careers, the average marriage age ends up going up, while the marriage rate also drops, so the population is bound to decline.

Hiroshi: In a rural part of South Korea, most men's wives are from other countries in Asia.

Ryoichi: Which ones?

Hiroshi: Vietnam, Thailand, Malaysia, all over.

Ryoichi: There is more freedom in South Korea than I thought.

Hiroshi: There are problems there, too, but they seem to be pretty practical about it. Measures to raise birth rates are somewhat effective, but in the end there is a limit to what they can achieve. Furthermore, achieving a massive rise all at once is extremely difficult.

One of the reasons the birth rate remains so low in Japan is because the age at which people are getting married has risen by around 10 years. Thirty years ago, about 80 percent of women were married by the time they hit 30. Now that number is just under 20 percent. The birth rate among married women has hardly changed, but the rate at which women are getting married has dropped. Maybe women are not interested in getting married because there are too many fun things to do with their time these days. [laughs]

Ryoichi: Ultimately, Japanese women probably still want to start a family and have children, but they face the dilemma of having to choose either their career or their family.

Hiroshi: Japanese society has started resembling that of Northern Europe in that maternity and child care leave are now acceptable. The issue, however, is whether Japan can maintain the size of the labor force under such a system. The Abe administration has proposed a three-year child care leave system, but frankly speaking, making such a system viable requires tremendous work on the part of both the company and the employee. Still, quite a number of women at Rakuten return to work even after taking three years of child care leave, so I guess it varies for each person. However, even if women are able to return to the workforce after they give birth, I doubt this solves Japan's labor shortage.

Ryoichi: After all, we have to raise the birth rate.

Hiroshi: It would be great if we could raise the birth rate, but right now it looks like it will be difficult to get the birth rate over two children per couple.[3] Even if it successfully rises to two, Japan's population would still be shrinking. Among the OECD countries, only the United States has a growing population. The reason the U.S. population is growing is because of the rise in its Hispanic

---

[3] The World Bank shows that the birth rate in Japan has held steady at 1.4, http://data .worldbank.org/indicator/SP.DYN.TFRT.IN.

population; the Caucasian population is increasing, but its share is declining.

Ryoichi: Why does Japan refuse to accept immigrants?

Hiroshi: I guess the Japanese are quite closed off to outsiders.

Ryoichi: I believe immigrants in Japan can be largely divided into two groups. First, you have those who enter Japan as inexpensive workers who perform the same jobs as the Japanese for lower wages. Second, you have immigrants with special skills. In the latter case, you have special talent entering Japan in the form of workers with expertise or technical skills that are not found in the Japanese workforce. From an international trade perspective, not only do you have a movement of people, but you have a subsequent movement of technology and expertise as well, which is extremely important.

For those reasons, I am, in principle, in favor of immigration. On the other hand, while the acceptance of inexpensive laborers from abroad may produce short-term benefits thanks to their low wages, this also creates a variety of social problems. Economically, things might not add up if the cost resulting from these problems is very high, and thought needs to be put into how to keep track of that. I am sure there are tons of foreign workers who want to work in Japan, so this is quite a troublesome issue.

Hiroshi: I believe we are living in an age where having diverse values and cultures is very important. As information becomes globalized thanks to the spread of the Internet, the Japanese model of developing technology independently inside Japan and packaging this into products to be sold abroad is no longer valid. It is now time to recognize the importance of diverse values, invite all kinds of people into Japan, interact with one another, and share ideas to make the economy grow.

The same applies to Rakuten. The company cannot be managed by Japanese alone. That is why I believe we should discuss how to maintain the great things about Japanese society, be it Japanese culture or Japanese traditions, while promoting internationalization.

Summary

- Revise the system of lifetime employment, and foster a dynamic and mobile workforce.
- Introduce a white-collar exemption.
- Hire foreign workers for fields such as nursing and child care.
- Draw the world's best and brightest to Japan.

3

The Power in Questioning Abenomics

History of Abenomics

Hiroshi: I selected innovation and operational capability as the pillars of my "Japan Again" proposal in line with the Japan revitalization strategy. These are closely related to the growth strategy, which is the third of the three arrows of Abenomics. I would like to talk about the first and second arrows of Abenomics: bold monetary policy and fiscal policy. Let's start with a broad discussion of Abenomics.

At the Japan Association of New Economy's Abenomics Forum in June 2013, Professor Heizo Takenaka of Keio University said that Abenomics was 100 percent correct. Robert Feldman of Morgan Stanley MUFG Securities has also praised it highly, calling it a grand slam. As an economist, how do you feel about it?

55

Ryoichi: I think Prime Minister Abe is currently steadily advancing and implementing his plan. I believe he possesses excellent political acumen.

Hiroshi: Perhaps he learned from the failure of the first Abe administration. I know of a certain start-up firm in the United States that failed at its first launch attempt, losing all of its four billion yen [$40 million] in funding. But the second time around, the same investors all gave just as much as they did the first time.

Ryoichi: Up to this point, banks have been very sensitive to the attitudes of the Bank of Japan and Ministry of Finance when investing in companies. They have not been favorable to investments in risky businesses. We do not have as many individual investors here as they do in the United States. I think Japanese people tend to be risk averse, and, accordingly, banks and securities firms are also safety-focused. I think this presents a tremendous obstacle to the liberalization of the financial sector in Japan.

Hiroshi: In the United States, investors play the role of sources of investment for venture or start-up firms that also raise economic efficiency and innovation. But in Japan, the main source of investments is from banks. And above the banks is the Financial Services Agency, whose commissioner reports to the Minister of Finance, which controls the banks, regulating the flow of funding.

Ryoichi: In the United States, the Department of the Treasury is independent of the agencies regulating finance. The independence of the Bank of Japan's fiscal policy is important in Japan, too. That is something that I want to specifically say to Prime Minister Abe. I think it is fine for economists to come out in favor of Abenomics. The problem is the extent to which Prime Minister Abe understands monetary and fiscal policy. Because the economy is currently experiencing deflation, he is first trying to steer it back on course and return it to a safe speed, as well as establish a 2 percent rate of inflation. The question is whether the Bank of Japan will be able to put on the brakes when the speed at which the economy accelerates has increased. That point is what I am most concerned about.

Hiroshi: It feels like there is a heavy atmosphere in the mass media such that no one seems able to criticize Abenomics. Japan may currently be turning back toward state capitalism. I've heard from an editor at a major newspaper that an article he tried to write raising critical points about Abenomics was killed by the leaders of his paper. However, Prime Minister Abe said in an address, "Mr. Mikitani, you are always trying to provoke controversy. Keep doing that." [laughs]

Ryoichi: There was an academic named Karl August Wittfogel, who was active prior to World War II. He argued that Japanese people stick together because we have a culture of rice cultivation. He believed that because people needed to manage the water of a wide area of rivers and ditches in order to cultivate rice, the rice-farming people of Asia have a tendency to group together. It may be that the choice of not expressing our opinions and not criticizing others is in our DNA.

Hiroshi: It is often said that monetary policy must be independent or that central banks must be independent, but what is the reasoning behind that?

Ryoichi: Put simply, to protect against inflation. No matter how the agency in charge of financial policy does it, when the government spreads funding throughout an economy to try and improve it, it tends to cause inflation. It has been proven historically that if there is force behind fiscal policy, it will cause inflation. For that reason, the biggest issue for the Bank of Japan, being in its central position, is to calmly steer the economy to suppress inflation. That the central bank should be independent from fiscal policy and work to suppress inflation is a commonly shared idea throughout the world.

That said, the bank's job is complicated during an economic downturn. Even during times when fiscal policy causes the government to incur debt, there is still a need to implement measures to stimulate the economy. It is an extremely delicate problem. If the Bank of Japan had the attitude that it was ready to offer as much money as the government thought was needed, then there is the risk that we would see inflation. But then again, if they close the spout of funding too tightly, the economy will suffer. For that reason, this is a problem no matter what country we might talk about.

Those in charge of fiscal policy issue government bonds to provide funding, and critical to this discussion is the issue of how much they moderate that funding. Or to raise another issue, if money is borrowed for financing to stimulate the economy, when the economy improves there is a need to return that money, but if, regardless of that, the economy improves and the government does not pay its debt but continues to spend, then the scale of fiscal policy expands. This, too, has been a problem for every country around the world for a long time.

We are currently in a deflation period, and I also approve of the idea of issuing government bonds to stimulate the economy, because I believe that if we do not enhance the instantaneous speed of the economy, we will not be able to recover from deflation. And then there is the issue of the fundamental importance of judging what sort of state the Japanese economy is in and whether deflation is continuing or whether we have already recovered.

Looking at the state of the Japanese economy in terms of a longer, 10-year span, have we already escaped deflation, or are we still overcoming it? We know that the speed of the economy has increased, but the point of whether we have actually recovered from the period of deflation is going to be the most important issue from now on as we consider fiscal or monetary policy.

Independence in Finance

Hiroshi: Monetary theory was originally your specialization, wasn't it?

Ryoichi: When I was a professor in the economics department at Kobe University, I taught a course on U.S. economic theory. I taught a total of four blocks: separate classes and separate seminars once a week to under-graduate and graduate students. I explained the kind of monetary, fiscal, and economic policies undertaken by the United States after World War I; offered analysis on how economists in the United States view those policies; and lectured on whether they had developed theories based on those experiences. When I wasn't lecturing, I was usually in my office, engrossed in research.

Hiroshi: What sort of research did you do, specifically?

Ryoichi: One theme that I put a lot of effort into was an attempt to empirically verify the effect that monetary policy has on the real economy. Another topic was a consideration of the debate around Keynes' monetary theory of interest. There was a lively debate going on then about whether interest rates were decided based on the stock of currency in existence or based on the flows of capital as well as supply and demand and so on. I analyzed both sides of that debate.

The third topic I researched involved an analysis of money flow, which I did in order to grasp, statistically, the way in which capital flowed in line with financial transactions, focusing on the central banks of each country. I pursued research on that topic as well.

Hiroshi: In what form did you present your results?

Ryoichi: I wrote papers and submitted them to academic and economic journals. In terms of academic societies, I mainly presented to the Japan Society of Monetary Economics.

Hiroshi: You did a lot of empirical research.

Ryoichi: There are economists who focus only on theory, but I have always felt that theory alone is meaningless. We need to always follow the workings of the real economy and work the data into how we view and formulate our theories. That was the policy of the government as well in the past, and so I interacted widely with the staff of the Bank of Japan Research and Statistics Department and economists involved with the Ministry of Finance, who were all also members of the Japan Society of Monetary Economics. I am glad that we were able to exchange information. When I wanted to look into data on something, it would often take me one or two days to find the data I was searching for if I looked on my own, but a call to one of my close friends at the Bank of Japan or in the government could help get me the data right away. I treasured those relationships.

I served as the president of the Japan Society for Monetary Economics for many years, and was the chairman from 1994 to 1998. When I was the chairman, we actively pursued many creative initiatives, such as the holding of joint symposiums with other academic societies and the Bank of Japan. I remember those times fondly.

Hiroshi: Around when did the independence of monetary policy become a problem?

Ryoichi: That was around when I was still at the Japan Society for Monetary Economics in 1998. It was related to the issue of the revision of the Bank of Japan Act. Back then, the independence of the central bank in regulations was clarified. During the period of high-speed growth at the end of the war, there was a lot of funding available and no problems, but we needed to have separate monetary and fiscal policies in case the economy takes a downturn. In Japan's case, there was the risk that the independence of monetary policy would be threatened by the Ministry of Finance working to suppress the Bank of Japan.

Based on the grounds that collusion between the agencies in charge of monetary policy and fiscal policy could lead to inflation, we economists gave our views on the development of the insistence that the independence of the Bank of Japan and central banks in general be maintained. However, the Bank of Japan took advantage of that and became conceited. It was really unfortunate; a lot of us felt that we had not insisted on independence just so the Bank of Japan could act in an arrogant way.

Hiroshi: This time the Bank of Japan has substantially changed its policies and is starting to pursue an active policy of monetary easing that is different from the past in both its scope and reach. How do you feel about that?

Ryoichi: The Japanese government and Bank of Japan have been paralyzed up until now by the trauma of inflation caused by the lack of an independent monetary policy. Regardless of that, the Bank of Japan should have implemented more active policies in the past. That is why it is such a game changer for the bank to implement the easing that is different from the past in both its scope and reach under the new system being led by Governor

Haruhiko Kuroda. There is one thing that I feel I must take this opportunity to say: I wish the general public would take more interest in monetary policy.

The Optimal Inflation Rate

Hiroshi: When I asked a politician from the Democratic Party of Japan (DPJ) about the easing that is different from the past in both its scope and reach, which is set to ensure inflation of 2 percent in two years, he said that it would be better to use the target of 1 percent that his party had called for. I'm not a macroeconomist, so I cannot judge the theory of inflation targeting, but I do have the feeling that it is at least a good thing that we are moving in the right direction, away from the period of deflation and a strong yen. There are those in academia who are saying that 2 percent is an unrealistic target. What do you think?

Ryoichi:　Theses about what the most appropriate rate of inflation is are something that monetary policy societies inside and outside of Japan have been debating for a long time. It is the most important theme of monetary policy theory.

There have been many hypotheses. For example, Milton Friedman of the University of Chicago argued that zero percent was the most appropriate rate. But because the current system includes a mechanism for inflation that is tied to rises in certain costs, it is not easy to reach zero percent inflation. For instance, the labor market just isn't in a state of perfect competition—there are labor unions and so on.

So given that the market is not in a state of perfect competition—and considering what sort of inflation would be good by looking at the trends in the U.S. and

Japanese economies after World War II—I have come to the conclusion that only mild inflation could lead to a good outcome.

The theory of inflation targeting, which encourages inflation by setting a certain target for inflation, emerged as an extension of the discussion I just mentioned. The biggest problem is determining what percentage the inflation rate should be set at so that we don't fall into the vicious cycle in which prices go up when wages go up and wages go up when prices go up.

I have done some research on that point. To the extent that I have seen in the economies of the United States and Japan after World War II, I believe that around 2 percent may be a good annual rate, both historically and experientially. Above that level there will be an increase in wages, and the increased cost to businesses will be reflected in prices, moving us in a bad direction.

The topic of what is the "most appropriate" interest rate is a compelling one. There is a big difference between 2 percent and 3 percent. At 2 percent, we may reach a certain balance in the economy. At 3 percent to 5 percent, however, expectations of inflation will rise swiftly, inflation will lead to more inflation, and then once we pass a certain line, all will accelerate, and the balance we once had will be destroyed in one fell swoop. That is my opinion based on experience.

Another issue worth considering is how we think about inflation after a period of continued deflation. For example, say that deflation continues for four years; unless we push inflation sharply up to 8 percent, we will not be able to achieve the inflation target of 2 percent per year. That's a big problem.

Hiroshi: I think side effects also arise from inflation.

When the national debt is one quadrillion yen, a rise of

2 percent in the real long-term interest rates will cause the cost of interest rates to rise by 20 trillion yen. It makes you want to throw your hands up in despair. [laughs]

Ryoichi: That's exactly right. The size of the national debt is too large. But consider how the real long-term interest rates are decided. It involves the extent to which we can increase productivity and how far we allow the interest rate to rise. So if productivity rises, even if monetary easing is done, there should be a damper on the rise in prices. For that reason the organization in charge of national finance needs to be thorough in its analysis of the future and steer the macroeconomy well.

Hiroshi: So if there was an explosive improvement in productivity, could there be an increase in real income even if the inflation rate was zero percent?

Ryoichi: Yes. That's correct.

Hiroshi: In that case, I start to have doubts about whether the nominal inflation rate is really that important.

Ryoichi: The thing is, if the inflation rate actually was zero, there would be an increase in unemployment. We need to have mild inflation.

Hiroshi: So monetary easing really is the key to achieving inflation targets.

Ryoichi: Yes, monetary easing.

Hiroshi: But in that case, if interest rates fell, financial institutions would receive less income than they expected. I suppose it would make it difficult for them to operate.

Ryoichi: That could happen. Because people cannot make money by lending out at low interest rates, we do see a situation in which lenders stop giving money to corporations.

Hiroshi: In that case, the economy would be good, but the financial institutions wouldn't make any money. If a sudden rise in interest rates occurred in such a situation,

I wonder if there wouldn't be a large risk of sudden inflation.

Ryoichi: That's true, I think. Expectations toward inflation are not something that changes gradually over a month or so. They change suddenly whether they are rising or falling. Because the level of expectations changes suddenly, organizations in charge of monetary and fiscal policy really get to show what they are made of when faced with the challenge of how to deal with shocks.

Halting the Rise of Interest Rates

Hiroshi: Is it even possible to achieve what the Abe administration is trying to do? Is it possible to suppress a rise in interest rates while producing inflation? That is a point worth discussing.

Ryoichi: The only way to suppress a rise in interest rates is through credit rationing.

Hiroshi: What's credit rationing?

Ryoichi: Interest rates usually rise in relation to supply and demand, but suppose that we keep interest rates low at that time. If interest rates are low, you may get a situation in which you have gathered 10 trillion yen to loan out but you receive requests for 20 trillion yen. In such cases, the financial agency may tell the groups charged with the exclusive rights over government spending that they should lend out the money because investment is extremely important, and the funds may then be portioned out.

Hiroshi: If interest rates are low, I wonder if investors raise the funds in Japan and use them abroad?

Ryoichi: Investors may indeed go overseas.

Hiroshi: The Abe administration is considering a reduction in tax on capital expenditures to address the problem that such expenditures to create or improve factories are low in Japan. But thinking from the perspective of a business leader who would be doing the actual investment, I feel that rationally I can wait on investments if the current high stock price and weak yen situation continues for a bit longer. The situation is extremely opaque.

Ryoichi: The problem with giving companies a tax break to allow them to make capital expenditures is that it is extremely difficult to evaluate whether each company is using the extra funds to actually make such expenditures. If governments are going to give tax breaks for capital expenditure, then they must keep their eyes open and carefully evaluate just how close the relationship between the financial agency and the industry in question has been up until this point.

Hiroshi: In that sense, it may be better to lower taxes in a consistent way. There is also the point that tax revenue can increase as a result of a decrease in tax rates. I'm not a specialist in monetary theory, so I can't really say anything in respect to an evaluation of the easing, which is different from the past in both its scope and reach. I am very skeptical about one point, though, which is whether the funding freed up through monetary easing will become investments. If those funds are not used for investments, then I wonder if a lack of incentives toward domestic investments exists in the first place. Having an insufficient workforce isn't the only problem. There are also a variety of regulations, and taxes are high. Aren't those the actual reasons why funds aren't used for investments?

In that case, even if companies that have lost their competitiveness—such as those in the consumer electronics industry—invest, the only result will be a greater burden for them to bear. I think, in the first place, the topic of conversation should be, what do we do once there is a recovery of competitiveness? Regardless of the extent of monetary easing, the main actors will always be companies. I believe that if there isn't a simultaneous improvement in the efficiency of company management, along with greater trust in the strength of the Japanese economy, there will not be an increase in investments.

Important to this as well—although it is a roundabout way of tackling the issue—is the need for education reform. There are great expectations that education in Japan will change and that Japan will change from that. To that end, I believe we must invest in education and create visible measures to improve English capabilities. All of this, including my proposal for the IT autobahn concept, feeds into what I see as our need to invest in next-generation information infrastructure.

What to Do About Our 1-Quadrillion-Yen Debt

Hiroshi: On another financial topic, hasn't the per capita debt of the citizens of Osaka swelled to around 1.7 million yen?

Ryoichi: Yes. Plus the debt of the Osaka Prefectural Government.

Hiroshi: The total debt is 4.9 trillion yen divided by approximately 2.9 million people, making the per capita debt 1.7 million yen. And apart from our debt, the government of Osaka continues to spend as much as it wants. [laughs] The question now is, who can pay back that tremendous debt?

Still, the debt of the national government is an order of higher magnitude. The total debt is approximately

1 quadrillion yen—more than two times the GDP. It is such a large debt that you want to throw your hands up in despair. If the country were a company, it would not be double profits, but a debt two times the entirety of sales. That level of debt is quite difficult to repay.

Ryoichi: How would you propose this problem be resolved?

Hiroshi: I would create a grand design, set goals, and work toward reducing costs. I think there are two ways of going about it: (1) We can reduce the debt in proportion to the GDP, or (2) we can reduce the debt by setting a monthly limit on the per capita costs associated with each citizen. We can reduce costs without lowering the quality of policies by using IT. I will explain that more fully in Chapter 4, but I will say now that I believe a centralized governmental system is a high-cost system. Just in the way that a corporation can lower costs by creating subsidiaries, is there not a need for the state to advance decentralization? By doing so, it would be possible to integrate entrepreneurship into state management. Public employees have certain unwritten privileges. They never suffer pay cuts and they are never fired. I believe that we need to destroy these privileges. What do you think?

Ryoichi: Put simply, the solution is mild inflation, as I touched on earlier. If we return all of the large debt at once, the economy will crash. I think it would be better if we could absorb the debt through mild inflation. Luckily, the people of Japan are inclined toward savings and tend to have high savings. Unlike the countries of Europe that owe debts to other countries, most of the government bonds issued by our government are purchased domestically. Then again, we can't continue to issue national bonds without limit. We have to think about applying the brakes somewhere.

Hiroshi: Because most of the purchasers of national debt are Japanese citizens, there are those who believe that the situation is better than the one faced in the United States. However, some are also saying that things being what they are, national finances will not be sound until we raise the consumption tax to around 27 percent. To the extent that I have spoken with politicians here, I don't believe that they really have much of a long-term vision. I think it was different when the Liberal DPJ was in power over such a long period, but now all they think about is the next election.

Ryoichi: Your own election is an important one, of course.

Hiroshi: An issue for them is always whether they can win elections, so I don't think much can be done about it in a way, but I also think this is dangerous. The dominant opinion in society right now seems to be that it doesn't matter how much debt we have as long as the economy improves.

Ryoichi: That is certainly dangerous.

Hiroshi: The Ministry of Finance is naturally thinking about what will happen if things continue as they are. The grim truth is this: Even if we say that competitiveness is the source of economic vitality, nothing can be done if we don't have the money to accomplish anything. From the perspective of the Ministry of Finance, their job is to safeguard the nation's money, but they end up giving out that money because of political pressure.

Ryoichi: Conversely, what could we do even if we didn't have any money? I think just about the only option would be regulatory easing.

Hiroshi: Politicians are leading the Ministry of Finance. If political control comes to be exerted over the Bank of Japan, which should play an oversight role in all of this, there will be no limit to the dangers we could face. We must have a system of checks and balances.

Ryoichi: The importance of the independence of the Bank of Japan has already been proven.

Hiroshi: It is the only function of balance in the economy. But the viewpoint of politicians is nevertheless very shortsighted.

Ryoichi: Above all, to the next election we go. [laughs]

Hiroshi: That may be the effect of the single-seat constituency system. In the past, even if you said things that people didn't really like, you could still win a seat by being second or third in an election. But now, because people must come out on top, we have seen the emergence of populism that panders to public opinion. And for that reason, no matter how large the national debt grows, the party that improves the economy will win elections.

The Pros and Cons of Abenomics

Hiroshi: Today I had a meeting with some businessmen here in Osaka. It left a big impression on me. Many of them voiced concerns about the future. They wondered about the wisdom of pursuing such large-scale changes in monetary policy. They worried about what might happen if interest rates rise.

Many people out there view fiscal stimulus with skepticism. There are too many policies with a low multiplier effect, and they question whether it will be effective even if they invest. For example, the budget for reconstruction in the areas affected by the Great East Japan Earthquake of 2011 has been set at 25 trillion yen, and I can think of many uses for that money that wouldn't please anybody except the construction industry. Concerns remain about the effects of fiscal stimulus.

Regardless of what sort of reconstruction budget is really needed, I do believe that it is extremely important that we stick to our budget when carrying out a fiscal stimulus, whether it be for the expansion of runways at Tokyo International Airport, the creation of an information and communications network that would be affordable for households using fiber-optic cables, or investments into education.

Ryoichi: Yes, I hold the same opinion.

Hiroshi: We need investments in hardware, so there has to be a budget for earthquake countermeasures, but I think the main point of how we perceive whether a policy really has a multiplier effect is extremely opaque. That is my impression anyway.

Ryoichi: As you know, a major problem in economics is figuring out how big the multiplier effect is when the government makes an investment.

$$1/(1 - \text{marginal propensity to consume}) = K$$

The multiplier in this equation is represented by K. This is a theory advanced by Keynesian economists. So for example, if a person consumes half of their income, their *consumption propensity*—in other words, the amount of their income that goes toward consumption—is 0.5.

In such a case, the multiplier, K, would be 2. Here, the multiplier effect is shown to increase the input by two times. But in reality, in times of economic trouble, even when there is income, not much of it goes toward consumption. So a great amount is taken off that multiplier effect of 2, and it ends up being closer to 1.

During times of economic downturn, fiscal stimuli are implemented for public works as a measure to boost the economy, and, in doing so, the unemployed are hired and begin to work. But because there is a downturn, there continues to be a strong tendency toward thriftiness throughout society, and, as such, the money people earn is not spent, but saved. So when implementing a fiscal stimulus, should we first invest in the construction of public works, or should we invest in communications infrastructure and education? Depending on which choice the government makes, the impact on the multiplier is very different. This is not just an issue in Japan; this same principle can be applied anywhere.

In the case of the areas of Tohoku affected by the Great East Japan Earthquake, where many of the affected people are incurring debts in order to rebuild their lives, even if the government uses national financing to build public works, if the revenue is eaten up by repayments on debts and doesn't transfer over into consumption, then the multiplier effect will be close to zero. Even if it isn't zero, I don't think it will be very big.

Hiroshi: This is not just about consumption by individuals, though. What will happen to the entire economy? Does fiscal stimulus have an effect of increasing the rationality of the economy?

Ryoichi: What do you mean by the rationality of the economy?

Hiroshi: For example, if you build expressways, the efficiency of logistics increases, and so the multiplier effect increases as well—that sort of thing.

Ryoichi: What is invested in depends on the concrete policies of the government at that time, so there is an absolute need to check on the way taxes are being used.

Furthermore, I believe that we should involve the local residents who are being affected by the investments, and not just leave it up to government officials and construction companies. For instance, in the affected region of Tohoku, the people living there ought to know better than anyone else what that region needs right now. I worry about whether the government is checking with them or not.

Hiroshi: The thing is, building an expressway in an urban center where there would be a lot of people to use it has a different effect than building the same expressway in a depopulated area where there are almost no people who would use it. How does economics think about that?

Ryoichi: The first thing that Keynes ever proposed was that it didn't matter where the government spent money as long as it spent money. [laughs]

Hiroshi: So I've heard.

Ryoichi: Keynes wrote that in *The General Theory of Employment, Interest and Money*. He overstated the effect of employment, and I think when making an investment in a public work—and I am including education here—whether you invest in hard or soft infrastructure, there is an enhancing effect for productivity. In that sense, it is important to sufficiently take into account the opinions of the local residents, regional municipal governments, and researchers before deciding on a policy of fiscal stimulus. And this raises the question of who should check that. If it were up to me, I would say leave it to public opinion.

Hiroshi: Have any economists theorized about how fiscal stimulus connects to rises in productivity?

Ryoichi: There has been a debate in the United States about what kinds of public works investments are effective, so I believe there must be papers on that.

Hiroshi: My point is, if we are building an expressway that no one is going to use, wouldn't it be much more meaningful to invest in information infrastructure or the budget for education? What do you think?

Ryoichi: I agree. There can't be investments only in hard infrastructure like expressways, public works projects, and machines at factories; it is also extremely important to invest in soft infrastructure like education. However, when you invest in soft infrastructure, you are investing in people, so you do not immediately see an effect. There is a time lag between the investment and the effect, and, furthermore, the effect is difficult to see. For example, with education, you don't know if the teacher isn't skipping out on classes. [laughs] Figuring out how to check on things like that is a problem.

Hiroshi: When building an expressway, however, the government first needs to secure the land for that, and the whole process from the purchase of the land to completion can take decades, while an investment in education shows an effect in five to ten years, which I think might be called a short period of time.

Ryoichi: That's true. The younger children will graduate after five to ten years, but because you cannot see the effect, it is difficult to measure.

Hiroshi: The return on that investment is definitely difficult to see. However, I believe the slogan created for the policies of the DPJ is correct: "From concrete to people." But I think this policy shift was implemented by the DPJ in their own way, and as a result the primary balance got worse and worse. I think it's crucial to think about how we consider the primary balance, even when investing in people.

Summary

- Recognize that the independence of the Bank of Japan is indispensable to fiscal policy.
- Confirm whether the Japanese economy is truly recovering from deflation, and do not let this opportunity to shift monetary and fiscal policy go unutilized.
- Recoup fiscal debt through mild inflation (around 2 percent per year).
- Invest in communications infrastructure and education, which produce a large multiplier effect.

4

The Power of the Low-Cost State

The High Cost of Governance

Hiroshi: I want to discuss the high-cost structure of the Japanese government. I have given a lot of thought to the issue of cost structure. One of the biggest challenges to running a company is cost cutting for headquarters expenses, specifically personnel and administration costs.

At Rakuten, we have our headquarters, sales division, and development division, and within the headquarters are the accounting division and the office of the president, among other divisions. In order to cut our headquarters expenses, we established a key performance indicator (KPI) to keep overhead under 100,000 yen per employee.

A national government is roughly like the headquarters of a company, so it goes without saying that the lower the expenses, the better. I believe that an index is needed to show the best infrastructure that can be created at the lowest cost, but the government of Japan has never once considered this. Government officials only care about protecting their jobs, and they constantly search for ways to avoid anything that reflects negatively on what they've done in the past.

When trying to keep headquarters expenses in check, it's important to be closely aware of the expenses. The annual cost of providing government services in Japan in 2010 reached 23.1 percent of our GDP. Other developed countries like the United States and South Korea come in at 20.3 percent, while Germany is at 21.2 percent. The United Kingdom is higher than Japan at 25.3 percent, but Japan is still two to three points higher than South Korea, the United States, and Germany, making our government services costs as a ratio of GDP rather high.

This is precisely why the Japanese government needs to set a KPI to reduce annual government service expenses to 20 percent of GDP and consider ways to cut costs by 3 percent. If the government is advocating for corporate Japan to enhance its competitiveness, I say: first things first. The government needs to set an example by reducing its headquarters expenses. If it can't accomplish this goal, then government service expenses will only come back in the form of debt, so some thinking needs to be done about how to reduce these expenses to 20 percent of GDP. The problem is no such policy ever existed within the government.

Let's talk for a moment about corporate income taxes. Japan's corporate income tax rate stood at 35.64 percent as of January 2013, but when adding the special corporate tax for reconstruction on top of this, it becomes 38.01 percent, or the highest of any major developed country.

China's corporate income tax rate is 25 percent, South Korea's is 24.2 percent, and even Singapore is at 17 percent—all much lower than Japan. I have proposed that a KPI target of 25 percent be set for Japan's corporate income tax rate. As it stands now, I think just about every Japanese company will eventually be looking to leave Japan.

In addition, although business-to-business transactions were once considered the focus of the Internet, online business-to-consumer markets are now expanding as well. For example, a person purchasing goods from the United States for import to Japan isn't required to pay customs duties or consumption tax if the products are valued under a certain amount. Amazon was able to expand its market share so rapidly in the United States because it didn't have to pay state sales taxes [equivalent to consumption tax in Japan] on the sales of the products it sold from most locations when it first began selling goods online in the United States. Therefore, it was able to sell products for much cheaper. I predict that this kind of situation will occur on a much larger scale.

Ryoichi: I remember the issue with Amazon. I wonder if it's still free from paying state sales taxes.

Hiroshi: Amazon is now paying sales taxes in some states, but it didn't have to for about 15 years. It was a problem, but there was no solution, so the issue festered for a long time.

We offer media content and services in Japan, but consumers can now receive financial services from foreign firms as long as it's done over the Internet. That's what digitization means. Another issue is the way rules will be modified for the Trans-Pacific Partnership, exposing us to foreign firms and their ability to suck up everything around them. If we don't do something about this, there will soon be an exodus in which Japanese companies flee overseas.

Ryoichi: Or, the headquarters won't move offshore, but the essential tax base will, or the sales activities that incur taxes will.

Hiroshi: In addition to high corporate income tax rates, Japan is also plagued by overly expensive electricity costs. Some say the biggest reason for this is because of the huge cost of constructing and safely maintaining nuclear power plants. But I think the problem actually lies with regional monopolies. This is because companies with a market monopoly can easily raise rates. What's more, Prime Minister Abe is surrounded by the heads of power companies, other energy sector companies, and the Ministry of Economy, Trade and Industry (METI). This is why we've been hearing so much about the restart of nuclear power plant operations.

Ryoichi: That's terrible. This same structure can be found at the Kankeiren.[1]

Hiroshi: I can believe it. Simply put, this is all a ruse to pluck more hard-earned money from the people of Japan.

Ryoichi: Why hasn't privatization taken place in the power and gas sectors?

Hiroshi: The national government has said it will privatize these sectors. I have a feeling they will, but in the end nobody knows what will happen. Personally, I feel Prime Minister Abe's strong commitment to the separation of electricity production from distribution and transmission. The key to raising Japan's competitiveness lies with how efficient we can make our country. Said in simpler terms,

---

[1] Kankeiren (abbreviation of Kansai Keizai Rengokai, or Kansai Economic Federation in English) is one of Japan's representative economic organizations established in 1946, representing and realizing the collective will of the Kansai business community.

we need to avoid doing unnecessary things, liberalize markets, reduce headquarters expenses, and cut taxes. What kind of curve do you call it when taxes are lowered and tax revenues actually increase as a result?

Ryoichi: It's called a Laffer curve. This was a theory first advocated by U.S. economist Arthur Laffer, who showed in a graph that although tax revenues rise after tax rates are hiked, tax revenues conversely decline once the tax rate hits a certain number.

One of the things that stood out from what you said was that the cost of government services in Germany is lower than in Japan. Germany is often thought of as a country with a high-cost structure because of its high public utility charges, but even Germany has been able to keep its government service costs at 21 percent of GDP. I wonder if the people of Japan know that they pay much more for electricity and gas than other developed countries.

Hiroshi: I don't think so. That's why you need to publish this book! [laughs]

Ryoichi: No kidding. I think gasoline has also historically been more expensive in Japan. Is that still true today?

Hiroshi: That hasn't really changed from where I've been looking. The reason why gasoline is so expensive in Japan is because of the taxes. A provisional tax that is basically a gasoline tax [gasoline excise and local road tax] was in place to provide a tax base for road development and improvement, which effectively doubled the taxes. This became a hot topic in the National Diet [Japanese parliament] from 2007 to 2008, but a 53.8 yen gasoline tax is still applied for every liter of gasoline purchased to this day.

Ryoichi: Why aren't Japanese consumers more irate over their high taxes and costly public utilities? I think it may be because they believe Japan lacks resources and has to rely on energy imports, so there is nothing they can do about it but conserve and cut back. That's what I thought when I was younger.

Hiroshi: Japan's energy prices are higher than any other developed country, and among these the cost of utility gas is by far the highest. If Japan were set at 100, the price of utility gas would be 56 in the United States and 57 in the United Kingdom, or almost half as much as Japan. What's more, this data is from before the commercialization of shale gas production.

Ryoichi: Even utility gas prices in Germany would be 78 according to that scale.

Hiroshi: One of the main reasons behind this is the regional monopolies I talked about earlier. Japan has, plain and simple, pursued the wrong energy policy. One other reason why Japan has such high electricity prices is because liquefied natural gas (LNG) prices are linked to the price of oil. Japan's off-take agreements with oil-producing countries include a clause where the price of LNG increases whenever the price of oil rises. Only Japan is subject to this linkage.

Ryoichi: Is that the result of some kind of long-term agreement to secure a stable supply of oil, do you suppose?

Hiroshi: I'm sure that's the case. LNG prices today average around 4 to 6 yen per kilowatt hour on the open market, but Japan is paying 11 yen. The price of LNG has bottomed out since the worldwide emergence of shale gas, yet only Japan is being forced to pay these exorbitant prices. This is why our electricity prices are so high. They aren't high because we predominantly use nuclear power. In the end, Japan has been placed in this situation because of the actions of the METI.

How to Reform the High-Cost Structure

Ryoichi: Well, what do you think we should do to change the high-cost structure of the Japanese government?

Hiroshi: In my proposal, which I wrote from my perspective as a business leader, I advocate for making the public sector more efficient, reducing the number of public servants, and making full use of the national identification number system. The first thing I would do is reduce the number of public servants by half.

Ryoichi: If you did that would you still be able to attract the talent needed to administer Japan?

Hiroshi: I would raise pay to attract that talent. Japan's competitors include South Korea, the United States, and China, so trying to create a framework where we can beat our rivals is probably as hard as winning the World Cup, which is no easy task. If we are to accomplish this, I believe we need to put an end to the framework where public servants are employed and paid for life. I know it's unfortunate, but the salary of people with no market value must either be reduced or occasionally they must be let go. This is the way of the private sector, but, for some reason, public servants in Japan get the nonnegotiable guarantee of lifetime employment. In the United States, when a local government's finances are in dire straits, they even go so far as to terminate police officers. This is the way the public sector should have always been in Japan.

Ryoichi: But if you are going to introduce some kind of new IT, won't it really be hard to get rid of half the public servants in Japan?

Hiroshi: Today, the hottest topic in the United States is e-signatures. This would make it possible to digitize all public-sector documents, including resident registers, so people wouldn't have to go out of their way to head to city hall to obtain copies. Japan should be thinking of the same approach, but so far the government has shown absolutely no interest. At the very least, I feel it would be rather easy for a talented corporate manager to reduce Japan's cost of government services as a percentage of GDP from 23 percent to 20 percent.

Ryoichi: That means reducing the cost of government services to GDP by three points.

Hiroshi: Reducing the cost of government services to GDP by 3 percent would mean lowering the overall cost of the national government by about 8 percent. In other words, if today were set at 100, it would then be reduced to 92. Honestly, I feel that even that is being too soft. If it were really up to me, I'd cut that 100 to 50 without thinking twice about it. [laughs] Of course, doing this suddenly would raise employment concerns, so we would need to think of ways to address that issue. At the very least, the government should come up with goals to let us know which direction we are headed in.

Ryoichi: You also cite the need to lower the cost of health care and welfare services in your proposal. Does this also include online drug sales?

Hiroshi: In June 2013, the Abe administration announced plans to lift the ban on online sales of nonprescription drugs. This shows that the demands of private-sector members made it through, but we don't know how well this will go. I consider the bureaucrats to be a lot like zombies. [laughs] Even if they appeared to have lost 99 to 1, they can still multiply and make a comeback from that 1 percent. They always go on record saying that they'll consider something, but then they eventually tighten or expand regulations again.

Ryoichi: I see; they put it in writing.

Hiroshi: Here's how they do it: The key to the strategy is the
word "etc." A rather easy-to-understand example of this
is the issue of "TOEFL, etc." The third recommendation
of the Council for the Implementation of Education
Rebuilding is called *The Future of University Education, etc.*
It was issued in 2013. The title even includes the word
"etc." [laughs] The body of the text has the statement,
"Universities should utilize external certification exams
like the TOEFL, etc., during the entrance exam and
graduation approval process, and move forward with
educational programs taught in the English language, etc."
Including the "etc." means that they can dredge up the idea
of not having to use the TOEFL (Test of English as a
Foreign Language), but rather Galapagos-esque tests like
the EIKEN Test in Practical English Proficiency. Here it's
all about the way we interpret what the bureaucrats have
written. We can interpret it any way we like. Bureaucratic
talk—a language that few can understand—is satirically
known as "Kasumigaseki language," named after the
location of most government offices in Tokyo. When I
heard the discussions between politicians and bureaucrats at
the Industrial Competitiveness Council, I remember a
debate on whether to use "etc." there, too.

Ryoichi: Ah yes, "etc."

Hiroshi: They need to issue an order to ban the use of
"etc." in all bureaucratic language. [laughs]

Ryoichi: This is a form of deception that has been used by
bureaucrats for generations.

Hiroshi: I'd like to talk a little about health care and welfare
services. In Japan, the per capita cost of health care is
lower than it is in Europe and the United States. But we'll
need to actually lower this cost even more when you
consider how much Japan's population will gray over time.

Ryoichi: I agree with you 100 percent.

Hiroshi: Making health care and welfare services more efficient starts with information sharing through the proactive use of IT. The online sale of nonprescription and prescription drugs would make drugs cheaper and make it possible for consumers to purchase only the amount they need. This means that seniors wouldn't have to head to the hospital or pharmacy to fill their prescriptions and could receive their drugs without waiting too long. In this regard, the greater use of IT is a must.

Ryoichi: I wonder what the pharmaceutical industry thinks about the use of IT?

Hiroshi: Pharmaceutical industry groups probably couldn't care less about nonprescription drugs. Because those drugs really only represent a small market, valued at around 600 billion yen. They'd rather protect their core prescription drugs, and they're battling right now to set up a wall to prevent prescription drugs from being sold online. Once the ban on online sales of nonprescription drugs is lifted, the next logical debate will be whether to extend this to prescription drugs as well. This is why they are going all out to create negative stories about online sales of nonprescription drugs.

Ryoichi: Are prescription drugs that much of a money maker?

Hiroshi: Absolutely. The prescription drug market is valued at some 6 trillion yen, so there are huge profits to be made.

Ryoichi: Oh, really, I didn't know that. So the ones making the money are the drug makers, right?

Hiroshi: Actually the spoils here belong to the pharmacies and not the drug makers. I bet drug makers would welcome online sales, because they could reduce the margin they pay to intermediaries. The only work performed by pharmacies is following the order on the prescription and dispensing the drug. In the past, pharmacies used to mix actual drug compounds, but today I don't really see the need for them since all they do is dispense the drugs. Besides, mixing drug compounds is much more accurate, and hence safer, when done by a robot.

Addressing the Japanese Disease

Ryoichi: After hearing your explanation, I am reminded of something I mentioned earlier, which is that I think Japan may be in danger of catching a form of the British disease, one that we might call the Japanese disease.

Hiroshi: Simply put, the Japanese disease is the illusion that anything led by bureaucrats will go well and that the bureaucrats will save us if something goes wrong.

Let me share an anecdote I once heard from a British ambassador. The United Kingdom once privatized its railways, coal mines, and steelmakers because it felt they were the most important industries for the country. But they later found out that these industries weren't really that important at all. [laughs] As a result, the United Kingdom suffered for nearly half a century until Margaret Thatcher, the Iron Lady, came to power. I'm not afraid that Japan will develop the Japanese disease or a form of the British disease, because I know that we're already suffering from it.

Ryoichi: While that may be the case, the people of Japan have yet to notice. I think the British people were aware of their decline, but I wonder if the people of Japan think Japan is in decline. Some people may be aware of this, but it's even more dangerous when you don't notice your own symptoms. No one wants to know the details about their own illness, and it would be quite sad to see a country such as Japan that has worked so hard fall victim to an ailment like the British disease.

Hiroshi: The primary cause of the Japanese disease can be attributed to the protectionist policy of the METI. It is the remnant of antiquated policies known as the convoy system. These protectionist policies are what gave birth to our Galapagos syndrome. That is, Japan has created its own unique standards and nontariff barriers, essentially making it possible for only Japanese companies to succeed and thrive in the Japan market. The moratorium policies that I talked about earlier will deter the ability of Japanese companies to compete on the international stage. We may be in the midst of a vicious cycle. I'm not saying that we need to get rid of all of the government's industrial policies, but I believe the government needs to implement research and development (R&D) projects over the mid- to long term.

Ryoichi: I feel the same way. Many people seem to think that it's great if a researcher invents something, but they also seem to think that the researcher's involvement should stop there, and that the government should take the lead in R&D and commercialize the results. There are a lot of entrepreneurs in the United States making a lot of money from new technologies.

Hiroshi: Incidentally, I believe that government-led research and development should shift from a focus on subsidies-based aid to tax incentives. Subsidies involve the government providing funding if a company performs a certain type of research and development, so it doesn't carry much meaning for the market. Instead of handing out subsidies, I think it would be more beneficial if we applied tax incentives to R&D investments instead.

Ryoichi: But when we impose taxes, it's difficult to define exactly what constitutes R&D. Because R&D projects that mimic others shouldn't be eligible.

Hiroshi: Fundamental R&D requires huge sums of money and carries with it great risk, but it's absolutely essential, and for that reason it should be led by the government. Nuclear power development should have essentially been done by the national government. The semipublic, semiprivate process that was used lacked transparency and caused some rather strange results. Life science–related projects like induced pluripotent stem cells should be advanced through the leadership of the government as well. The other key point to mid- to long-term R&D is that it shouldn't be done by Japanese nationals alone.

Ryoichi: If foreign nationals came to Japan to be part of R&D projects, do you think they would find Tokyo easy to live in?

Hiroshi: I think they would.

Ryoichi: That's an important part of the equation.

Hiroshi: Fewer people want to go to China because of environmental pollution and concerns over food safety.

Ryoichi: For R&D, researchers will be living with their family, so I think it's important for the city to have a comfortable living environment.

Hiroshi: In that sense, Tokyo has great dining opportunities. It's safe and has friendly people.

Ryoichi: So, in terms of livability, Tokyo passes the litmus test.

Hiroshi: Yes. The only problem is English.

Ryoichi: What do you mean by the problem is English?

Hiroshi: Even if talented foreign nationals wanted to come to Japan, there is no work for them here. This is because they can speak English, but they can't speak Japanese.

Ryoichi: Oh, that's what you mean. I admit that in Europe they speak English in many companies. What's even more surprising is Sweden, where everyone on the street is actually speaking English to each other. Pretty much anyone under the age of 35 in Sweden is fluent in English. Seeing that, I came to think that this whole Englishnization thing you are doing is a good idea. Stockholm has a number of international schools, and foreigners have no trouble living there at all. Tokyo will need to step up language education and education for children, as well as become more open to new community members if it's going to open its doors to more foreign workers.

Hiroshi: The idea of a reduction in tax on capital expenditures for economic growth became a hot topic, even at the Industrial Competitiveness Council, but I think we're talking about a rather antiquated ideology. The one thing needed for competition, above all else—including manufacturing equipment—is intellectual property. We need to shift gears and find out how we can attract the world's best and brightest to bring their great talent and wisdom to Japan. The way things stand, it appears as if we're telling talent: "Don't bother coming to Japan." For example, only around 2,000 foreign nationals enter Japan with a technical visa each year.

Ryoichi: Wow, I didn't realize the number was so small.

Hiroshi: The United States is trying to increase their number to 300,000, when Japan is only accepting a mere 2,000. At first I thought that talent simply didn't want to come to Japan, but based on our experience hiring foreign nationals at Rakuten, we have found that Japan is fully competitive in the world marketplace as long as there is an environment set up in which they can work and the company pays the right amount of compensation. I think it would be harder to find a European who was willing to relocate to Silicon Valley in the United States.

Ryoichi: So, in that regard you think Japan would be a more attractive work destination for Europeans. I believe many Americans like Japan, but we have an even larger fan base in Europe.

Hiroshi: Rakuten is hiring people from around the world, and more than half our engineers are foreign nationals. One of our engineers in charge of Internet security is Russian and is one of the world's foremost hackers.

Ryoichi: Eh? Isn't a hacker someone who causes damage?

Hiroshi: No, he's one of the world's top five "white hat" hackers.

Ryoichi: Really?

Hiroshi: All of our engineers in our security unit, including him, communicate in English. Among our Japanese engineers there was one fellow who at first couldn't speak a word of English. He set his mind to studying English and decided from that very day to start speaking only in English during lunch and at break time.

Ryoichi: What do these foreign engineers think of Tokyo?

Hiroshi: They all say they really like it. America can be too individualistic, and it certainly isn't true that everything the United States makes is the best. They praise the positives of Japanese-style teamwork and our culture of hospitality. They also very much like the kindhearted nature of the Japanese people.

Ryoichi: Yes, that may all be true.

Hiroshi: There may have been discrimination in the past, but compared to other countries, I think there is less discrimination against foreigners in Japan today.

The United States and Individualism

Hiroshi: At the age of 29, when you were assistant professor at Kobe University of Commerce in 1959, you studied abroad in the United States on a Fulbright scholarship and through other funding, and you spent a total of two years and three months as a postgraduate student at Harvard University and Stanford University. After that, in 1972, at age 42, when you were a professor at Kobe University, you took our whole family to the United States and spent a year and nine months as a researcher at Yale University. You've also visited the United States on several other occasions since then. Based on your experience living over there, what is your impression of the United States?

Ryoichi: Based on my personal experience, I feel the United States is very much a country of individualism. Individuality is something that is heavily emphasized there. Which brings me to this point: If there is an idea, Americans really care about whose idea it is. At schools in Japan, you may get praised for answering something right based on the textbook. What stood out to me was that at schools in the United States, students are commended for sharing their unique opinions. When I was studying abroad at Harvard University, it was a given that we should share our own ideas, which made it a very positive experience.

Hiroshi: I think the fact that laws are named after individuals also shows the attention people pay to individualism. For example, the Americans have named their corporate reform act the Sarbanes-Oxley Act. The name of the law actually contains the names of the people who drafted it.

Ryoichi: The banking act that prohibited commercial banks from participating in the investment banking business, or the Glass–Steagall Act,[2] is another example of that. What I like about Americans is their straightforward nature. There's not much beating around the bush, and friends talk candidly to each other. I've had the opportunity to interact with many different people, including economists and people from the Federal Reserve Board, and I had very little trouble doing so.

Hiroshi: What do you think is the strength of the United States as a country?

Ryoichi: Well, I think they are just strong, period. [laughs] One more thing is, when the situation demands it, Americans become very patriotic. Perhaps it's because Americans have always enjoyed their freedom that they respond to behaviors of other countries that infringe on that quite intensely.

What has recently caught my interest is actually China. I was very curious as I watched the meeting in June 2013 between President Obama and President Xi Jinping at a private estate in Southern California, wondering what kind of discussion they were going to have. What was really interesting was that there happened to be maneuvers by the U.S. army in northern Okinawa during the time of the meeting. While it was not major news in Japan, I was relieved to learn that the United States had not neglected taking measures toward China.

Hiroshi: For the United States, the 1980s was a difficult period. It was when they even tried to learn from Japan's experience of reviving its economy following its postwar defeat and its "Japan as Number One" economic vision. I believe that was a turning point in the evolution of the United States. I admire the Americans' determination and clear-cut attitude. For example, Americans are okay with

---

[2]The Glass-Steagall Act was repealed in 1999.

the idea that their televisions aren't made in the United States.

Ryoichi: Maybe Americans think they would lose out if they insisted on using only domestically made products?

Hiroshi: Even Apple doesn't make any of its products on their own premises. This is probably based on the philosophy that the products that sell are ultimately chosen by the market itself. Also, I admire the Americans' willingness to learn humbly and overcome weaknesses.

Ryoichi: When I studied abroad in 1972, Toyota was first starting to produce auto parts at Atlas Fabric in California [currently, Toyota Auto Body California]. Toyota was considerate of the Americans it hired and taught them about Japanese-style flow production. This is how the Toyota Way spread in the United States. Toyota was very clever in its approach, but the Americans also showed their desire to learn something new with humility.

Hiroshi: However, I think the United States has a weakness when it comes to managing systems. That weakness was exposed during the bankruptcy of Lehman Brothers and the collapse of Enron before that. Another weakness is their health care system, which lacks universal coverage like in Japan. A little less than 20 percent of the population doesn't enroll in health insurance because they would be forced to pay for it individually out of pocket. In the end, this is part of the reason for the country's high health care costs.

Ryoichi: Americans think health care is up to the individual.

Hiroshi: I don't think individualism will always help them out. President Obama really had a hard time passing the Affordable Care Act through Congress.

Ryoichi: In the United States, the states hold all the power, so it may be difficult to pass policies for the entire country.

Hiroshi: Nevertheless, the Americans actually have dominance in the IT industry, so the country will be quite strong for some time to come. During their two-day meeting, President Obama and President Xi Jinping apparently talked about cyberterrorism and cybersecurity, but it would be more correct to say that the information they talked about is controlled by Google, not the United States. The CIA and other U.S. government agencies can access Google's information.

Ryoichi: In other words, inside information from China is being leaked out completely.

Hiroshi: I think they know everything. That's why China forced Google out of the country, to block access.

Up until now, competition has focused on manufacturing technologies, but going forward I think the relevance of competition through manufacturing technologies will fade away. That's because excess earning power from manufacturing technologies will decline. The only sectors where this remains is automobile and factory exports, but this excess earning power will gradually decline in all other sectors. Even in the realm of automobiles, there once seemed to be an unbridgeable gap between Toyota and Hyundai of South Korea, but now they are competing very closely. I think they are just about neck and neck today.

The Impotent Bureaucracy

Hiroshi: I'd like to talk about Japan's bureaucracy more. The bureaucracy is an intrinsic problem that inspired my proposals in "Japan Again." After the Democratic Party of Japan failed miserably in its attempt to dethrone the bureaucracy, Japan has reverted back to the belief that it's fine to have bureaucracy-led policies. This is a very dangerous situation. Giving control to the bureaucrats is the absolutely wrong thing to do.

The bureaucracy functioned well during Japan's period of high economic growth when there were clear policy targets, but today things are completely different. Globalization has advanced with the emergence of the Internet, bringing with it rising uncertainty. The cycle of innovation has been sped up immensely. Given this, if the bureaucrats are left in charge of industrial policy, we'll fall behind the world by two or three cycles. They roll out old ideas to great national fanfare, but Google's already been doing these things. [laughs] And they still invest in projects where Japan has no chance of winning, no matter how you think about it.

In the case of the METI, they conspire with the energy sector and related industries trying to protect the nuclear policy they've created for themselves. What's really symbolic [laughs] are the recommendations of the Industrial Competitiveness Council to include the use of nuclear power as a means to achieving economic growth. Do you have any concerns over Japan's bureaucracy?

Ryoichi: Okay, let me address Japan's bureaucracy. Internationally, bureaucracies have played an important role in the long-term development of many countries, such as the United Kingdom, Germany, and the United States. However, good bureaucracies have contributed to the development of a country and, conversely, bad bureaucracies have destroyed the vitality of a country. Although many academics, including German sociologist Max Weber, have debated this point, my question here would be: What conditions are needed for a bureaucracy to succeed?

The first condition is clear policy targets. When clear policy targets match the needs of the country, the bureaucracy is a good organization for efficiently achieving these targets. However, the story changes when that country is already among the leaders in the world. What to do then is really unknown territory, yet an actual target needs to be determined. In that case, the bureaucracy won't be able to define one—this will be a common problem no matter what country is discussed.

In the case of Japan, the postwar target was reconstruction, so everyone gave their best to rebuild the country. In this regard, the bureaucracy was very efficient, I think. However, about 20 or so years ago, Japan became one of the leading economies in the world. Ever since we've been in a position to choose our own path for the future, Japan's bureaucracy has only caused institutional fatigue. Therefore, I think we shouldn't be debating whether the bureaucracy is good or bad; instead, we need to think about how best to use the bureaucracy given our historical and social background.

The entity that can rightly control the bureaucracy is none other than the people. Politicians elected by the people play an important role, and the people who control those politicians play an even bigger one. The importance of this arrangement strikes home particularly when I see the recent moves made by Keidanren and in journalism.

Hiroshi: Keidanren doesn't have the perspective to move deregulation forward and revitalize Japan's economy. Frankly, it's become a kind of "old boys' club" that just protects the profits of companies with market monopolies. People often say that agricultural cooperatives and medical associations are organizations with vested interests, but I've recently started thinking that Keidanren is the largest of them all. Also, I'd venture to say that today Singapore is

the one country in the world with the most successful
bureaucracy.

Ryoichi: Ah yes, Singapore.

Hiroshi: The one unique thing about Singapore is its
political-appointee system, where top political leadership,
like the president and prime minister, appoint the top
bureaucrats. They select the heads of each government
agency from the private sector. The second thing I want
to mention about Singapore is that it uses separate
personnel evaluation systems for high-ranking officials and
for local officials. Essentially, they separate the bureaucrats
in charge of determining the country's strategy, who serve
almost as if they are part of a think tank, from the other
administrative public servants.

Ryoichi: However, corporate Japan always supports
Keidanren.

Hiroshi: You're right.

Ryoichi: Even if Keidanren members come from different
sectors, as long as they are representing major
corporations, Keidanren's interests are aligned with those
same major corporations'. The fundamental problem lies
within large private-sector companies. Japan's leading
companies mainly consist of manufacturers and trading
companies, but I wonder if these major corporations are
thriving freely on the world's stage in accordance with
their own principles of capitalism. Major corporations
are competing to survive. Yet, I have the suspicion
that corporate Japan colludes with and is supported
by the METI in an attempt to do everything the
Japanese way.

Hiroshi: In the case of the auto industry, which faces more
exposure to international competition, having national
policies is a must. In contrast, a few major corporations
are able to survive on the business of other major

corporations alone—I'm thinking here of companies like Tokyo Electric Power Company (TEPCO) or Nippon Telegraph and Telephone. At the top of the food chain are companies with a monopoly in their sector, and dangling below them are countless companies.

Internationalizing the Bureaucracy

Hiroshi: I feel like Toyota's Hiroshi Okuda and Canon's Fujio Mitarai stand out from the other chairmen of Keidanren throughout history, to an extent.

The problem with Keidanren is that it allows a bunch of companies with vested interests to get together and come up with standards and rules that apply only to Japan.

Ryoichi: To protect those interests, yes.

Hiroshi: When it comes to television broadcasting today, only Japan is in such an uproar about rolling out ultra-HD broadcast with 4K and then even 8K resolution. Smart TVs are now the mainstream around the world, so consumers are probably really wondering who on earth is going to watch such high-definition TVs. There was a media report awhile back about several commercial broadcasting companies getting together to block a commercial for Panasonic's smart TV, the Smart VIERA. When someone related to the story was asked why, they said that it was because if smart TVs take over, TV will become like the Internet, and no one will watch regular TV anymore. It's unbelievable.

That thought process was born out of an archaic Galapagos strategy in which companies only care about their home market and are reluctant to do anything else. The reason why the television broadcast industry in Japan has completely lost its market share in the world is because the Ministry of Internal Affairs and Communications and the METI took the lead in creating their own format and system that apply only to the domestic market.

Ryoichi: That's really the problem. The system has helped companies to reap benefits in Japan through market monopolies and oligopolies. But I think that time is already over, because the spread of the Internet is a game changer.

Hiroshi: Samsung of South Korea controls nearly 30 percent of the worldwide market for flat-screen TVs. It's a shocking statistic, and it makes you wonder whether Japanese companies should just stop making TVs altogether.

Ryoichi: If that were the case, they wouldn't be able to survive.

Hiroshi: Actually, they're just barely getting by as it stands now. What's even worse is the huge sums of money being provided to companies in the form of government subsidies.

Ryoichi: Yet the Japanese people, including myself, never get mad about that. [laughs] We really need to get angry. Journalists have a responsibility to notify the public about those things. This is really important. This is why Japanese journalists need to wake up to the truth. How is the bureaucracy acting now when there are no clear policy targets?

Hiroshi: Honestly, looking around, our bureaucrats aren't really good at what they do. They are blind to what's going on around them in the world today. Japanese business leaders aren't on par with their counterparts in the United States, while our bureaucracy is blind to the outside world. At the very least, I wonder if our leaders think we are okay with the way things are. The younger people under them are probably thinking we can't keep doing things the way we have been, but they can't argue with their superiors. [laughs]

Ryoichi: Maybe the actual people in charge are accurately analyzing the situation?

Hiroshi: Maybe so, but going back to television broadcasting, the world doesn't want ultra-HD broadcasts. Even Netflix, one of the United States' largest video-content providers, wants TVs that can view a lot of different media. They know that the world's markets don't want higher resolution. But the manufacturers here likely believe that if they block smart TVs from coming into Japan, they can sell their own 4K and 8K TVs. This Galapagos-like phenomenon is just like DoCoMo's i-mode, which ultimately caught on only in Japan.

Ryoichi: If there's a market in Japan, they can make it work somehow.

Hiroshi: In the past, Japan was able to beat out its peers with technology alone, but now even if you add together the market capitalization of Japan's top four home electronics companies, it's still less than half of Samsung's market capitalization. In this sense, Japan's bureaucracy should deregulate to the greatest extent possible and align Japan with international standards.

Ryoichi: Yes, I agree with you.

Hiroshi: Japan's bureaucracy wants to create standards that are unique to Japan at any cost. This holds true whether the sector is communications or broadcasting, because the most money can be made by this type of arrangement. But the other reason is that by creating their own standards, they increase their workload and justify their own existence. Because if they align everything with international standards, they'll be out of their jobs.

Sadly, though, they lack the ability at international conferences to make Japanese standards into international standards.

Ryoichi: It's just like the Japanese saying, "Every dog is a lion at home," meaning that they are tough on their own turf but shy outside of their own territory.

Hiroshi: One of the few achievements from the Industrial Competitiveness Council was adding TOEFL to tests for national public employees. This is very significant. However, the debate at the time moved to exempting bureaucrats who had already passed the test from taking the TOEFL. I wanted to say, "You're the ones who *should* be taking the TOEFL. [laughs] It's only English." They feel threatened even by English. But when it's all said and done we need to globalize the bureaucracy.

Ryoichi: I think some bureaucrats must be pro-globalization.

Hiroshi: Of course, there are some. These people are progressive thinkers. But then there is another problem, which is the infallibility of the bureaucracy.

Ryoichi: You mean the idea that bureaucrats never make mistakes?

Hiroshi: They can never critique what they've done. Whether it's nuclear power or our national debt. They hold on to their supposed infallibility at any cost.

Ryoichi: It's a fact that bureaucrats don't like being told they've made a mistake. This was the case many years ago when I was part of an advisory panel on postal matters. At the time, I witnessed the myth of bureaucratic infallibility with my very own eyes, as they didn't want to hear anything about errors, no matter how big or small. But the bureaucracy excels at efficiently controlling systems like the post office and telephone system, which they helped bring to every corner of the country. I think this is because bureaucrats are serious and earnest. At the very least, I felt then that they weren't the type of people who would lie to your face.

Hiroshi: But some of them haven't exactly been telling the truth recently, what with the pension fiasco at the Ministry of Health, Labour and Welfare and all. [laughs]

Ryoichi: Well, I came into contact with them some 30 to 40 years ago, but at that time I wouldn't have called them liars.

Creating Think Tanks

Hiroshi: What would happen if there were no bureaucracy? When I think about the great failure of the Democratic Party of Japan to remove the bureaucracy, I have to believe that the lesson here is that we need a control function as well as a brain function. One solution would be to create a think tank.

Ryoichi: Absolutely.

Hiroshi: Today, the Cabinet Office and Cabinet Secretariat are playing that role. But ultimately they don't have a packaged, comprehensive strategy. There's no clear overall strategy for where to cut costs and where to use money. In this sense, Japan lacks the ability to devise a national strategy.

Ryoichi: Although private-sector think tanks are pretty much nonexistent in Japan, the United States has many of them. For example, the Brookings Institution is a liberal think tank, and the American Enterprise Institute is a conservative counterpart. Whenever the Democratic Party is in power, the Republican brain trust is waiting in the wings. They're at a think tank working their best to come up with the next national strategy. I don't think that's the case with Japan.

Hiroshi: I think Keidanren has played a role in Japan similar to a think tank in the United States. I know I say this all the time, but heavy and chemical industries won't ever disappear. At the same time, Keidanren can no longer create the right strategies, because we've reached the time when heavy and chemical industries can no longer generate added value by themselves. So who's thinking about strategy? The top people at the Ministry of Finance probably are, but I don't think these people appreciate or understand the dramatic pace of change taking place in the world today.

Ryoichi: And that's why you're saying Japan needs a private-sector think tank.

Hiroshi: Japan does have a few think tanks, like the Japan Research Institute. It would be great if more people donated to these organizations, but unfortunately donations are coming up short.

Ryoichi: That's too bad, because the Toyota Foundation and others were doing a lot of great work.

Hiroshi: During the Koizumi administration, the Council on Fiscal and Economic Policy wielded a great deal of power and took on a lot of initiatives. The council was full of members who thought for themselves, including Hiroshi Okuda, former chairman of Keidanren; Professor Heizo Takenaka from Keio University; Jiro Ushio, chairman of USHIO; and Yoshihiko Miyauchi, chairman of Orix Corporation. The failure of the current Council on Fiscal Economic Policy can probably be attributed to the fact that very few of its members are corporate executives. Professor Motoshige Ito from the faculty of Economics at the University of Tokyo was a member, but he's not a businessman.

Ryoichi: How would you fix the bureaucracy? Where would you start?

Hiroshi: Well, the first thing would be to give more power to the Council on Fiscal and Economic Policy, since this time it was rather impotent. Heizo Takenaka should have been a member, but I hear the bureaucrats did everything in their power to avoid this.

Ryoichi: Things would have turned out differently if he were a member.

Hiroshi: Unlike the Industrial Competitiveness Council, which only has the power to research and deliberate, the Council on Fiscal and Economic Policy has legislative power.

Ryoichi: That may be the case, but the people of Japan still think bureaucrats are all-powerful, so the bureaucrats still have a relatively good amount of power. Therefore, the important thing will be how to inform the people about the truth when it comes to national finances and economic crises. Even with that information, the people support the bureaucracy.

Hiroshi: Even though bureaucrats are public servants? [laughs]

Ryoichi: You're right. In Japanese we'd say *koboku*, literally "public servant."

Hiroshi: Another important issue with regard to the bureaucracy system is political appointments. Essentially, I believe that senior officials in positions like director general and vice minister at government agencies and ministries should be hired from the private sector.

Ryoichi: I agree.

Hiroshi: Put another way, we need to create a framework through which talented human resources can work for the bureaucracy over five or ten years and then return to the private sector. So far, bureaucrats and the private sector haven't really mingled with one another for a variety of reasons. In the past, it was second nature for the two to mingle, but today that's not the case. Bureaucrats now have few opportunities to interact with businessmen, and for that reason they lack business savvy. They don't understand what's going on in the world around them. This is really unacceptable. It's why more executives with international track records need to be included in the Council on Economic and Fiscal Policy. A committee that will serve as the command center of this effort can be set up immediately.

Ryoichi: That may be possible, but does such a framework exist?

Hiroshi: Yes, it does. Yet, the current administration is simply making a lot of different councils, like the Industrial Competitiveness Council, the Council for Regulatory Reform, and others, to dilute control. In such a situation, the bureaucrats wield the most power. I feel that this approach is intentional.

Ryoichi: What do the bureaucrats want to accomplish personally? Is it all about climbing the bureaucratic ladder? [laughs]

Hiroshi: Oh, without a doubt.

Ryoichi: If all they want to do is be successful in life, then the problem lies with the definition of "success in life." Our generation grew up believing without question that climbing the corporate ladder was a good thing, but I don't think today's youth share that same belief.

Political Appointees

Hiroshi: I'm repeating what I've been saying, but the reason why Japan's bureaucracy has lost its way is the lack of political appointees. The ultimate goal of a bureaucrat right now is to reach vice minister or director general. This is why all senior bureaucratic leadership should be political appointees.

Ryoichi: It's a good idea.

Hiroshi: South Korean president Park Geun-hye filled more than half of her government's bureaucratic posts from the private sector. There is some debate about whether this is a good or a bad thing. It all depends on your point of view.

Ryoichi: We should just do away with the administrative vice minister system.

Hiroshi: My sentiments exactly.

Ryoichi: In the United States, all such posts are political appointees.

Hiroshi: At one time, Heizo Takenaka, a professor at a private university, served as a minister, so it's not like it's impossible in Japan. We should make all vice ministers political appointees. Doing so would help the bureaucrats focus on their actual work.

Ryoichi: I wonder if they'd really give up on their ambitions for advancement.

Hiroshi: Even the Bank of Japan governor is a political appointee. Any way you slice it, director generals and vice ministers should be made political appointees, and vice ministers should change each time the administration does.

Ryoichi: We really need to make a change there. Yet, we also need the support of the people and a sound legal basis for that change.

Hiroshi: When people are thinking only about promotions or getting ahead, they lose sight of everything around them. That's a fact. Even employees of Rakuten, which I would expect to have a more entrepreneurial mind-set, exhibit symptoms similar to the bureaucrats. This inevitably happens within any organization, and it's important to have a framework in place to root out that kind of behavior. I believe a political-appointee system is the best choice. We should legally require the appointment of private-sector people to the posts of director general and vice minister. I think if we would have done this, we would have never had to hear a comment from the Ministry of Health, Labour and Welfare as stupid as "we haven't calculated that in decades" during the pension scandal.[3] [laughs]

The other major problem is ministerial ordinances. Essentially, ministries can create their own legislation without going through the legislative process. This is how the dominance of bureaucrats has gone unchallenged for so long.

Ryoichi: But public servants would oppose any changes to this system or the elimination of ministerial ordinances.

Hiroshi: Yes, they would.

Ryoichi: They'd be vehemently opposed. They'd fight to the bitter end. You are talking about the elimination of one of their highest-profile jobs.

Hiroshi: But that framework is the reason why Japan has fallen behind. It's out of touch with the times. For example, take the prefectural license system for television broadcast stations. The system grants television broadcasting licenses by prefecture. It's only natural to think that this is ridiculous. [laughs] Go to any other country, and that kind of system wouldn't make any sense. It's the kind of thing that people have to ask to be repeated when they hear it, it is so unbelievable.

---

[3] A public scandal was created when the records of millions of social security pensions were not properly matched with individual pension identification numbers, thus making proper and full payment to social security recipients impossible.

What It Will Take to Improve the Bureaucracy

Ryoichi: Can you define a good bureaucracy? What about a bad one?

Hiroshi: As I said earlier, Singapore's bureaucracy can be considered a good one. I heard from a Singaporean that bureaucrats there are very well paid. They're paid the same salary as prominent business leaders and investment bankers. However, they're fired immediately for poor performance.

Ryoichi: So they're well-paid workers.

Hiroshi: It's not a seniority-based system, but a pay-for-performance one, so it's okay to have high wages. Conversely, if the positions were poorly paid, the bureaucrats would cling to their job titles. [laughs] If we're going to give more authority to high-ranking bureaucrats, then we should pay them well so they don't become attached to their titles.

Ryoichi: In the United States, the pay scale for the bureaucracy is low, but once they quit, they can expect a high-paying job in the private sector, like second in command at a bank.

Hiroshi: That's the same as what we call *amakudari*, the reemployment of retired bureaucrats to industries related to their public-sector work before their leaving the civil service. In the United States, this plays out in two ways: one where a bureaucrat is hired by the private sector and the other where someone from the private sector is hired to become a bureaucrat.

Ryoichi: In the United States, even people who are career bureaucrats within research bureaus are scouted by private-sector companies if they seem to have skills and talent. That's a little different from Japan. In Japan, bureaucrats are rehired based on their connections.

Whereas, in the United States, in the banking sector, a bureaucrat is hired based on his or her research and auditing skills. In other words, the process is entirely performance based.

With the Hispanic population increasing, the Democratic Party should be in control for some time, but once the current administration changes, all of the bureaucrats will be switched out.

Ryoichi: What will the Republicans do?

Hiroshi: Actually, I think now's the time for a change in policies. I think a leader who is more liberal on the topics of abortion and other issues will emerge from within the Republican Party. Once that person wins, the Republican Party may very well experience a renaissance.

Ryoichi: The Republican Party will continue to decline if they don't change.

Hiroshi: The problem is bureaucratic-centered state capitalism. The British disease is one of the more well-known ailments of this problem. What I mean here is that bureaucrats aren't smarter than the market.

I heard something interesting from a friend who is a senior manager at a government-affiliated financial institution. He pointed out that in Japan, the bureaucracy, industry, and financial sectors are basically all intertwined. The megabanks use their vast sums of money to buy favors from the government. This was the case with the bailout of Japan Airlines and TEPCO. They then gain huge economic interests from these favors, creating an endlessly repeating vicious cycle.

Let me use an example to describe what is happening with this. Say a major electronics manufacturer is to receive research grants from the METI equivalent to several percent of its sales. This is a huge amount of money. The prospect of it will cause the company to finalize R&D based not on what the market really wants, but on how it can get these subsidies from the METI. This is why it develops technologies that are completely unrelated to international market trends. In turn, it loses competitiveness and heads toward bankruptcy or a bailout over the long term.

That is why research subsidies need to stop. Research should be performed by academics. Companies don't need government handouts to fund their R&D. For example, Google doesn't receive a penny from the government. Corporate research subsidies are not only thrown away, but they also lead to the creation of moratorium policies. Such moratorium policies that extend the life of companies that should be left to fail is a major problem created by Japan's bureaucracy. Companies have life spans, and the ones that are failing should be allowed to fail.

Ryoichi: I agree with the gist of what you are saying. It's quite clear that Japan needs to graduate from its past and move forward in a new direction. However, my concern is how Japanese youth feel about this. I hear that most young people still want to work at major corporations. There may not be anything we can do about this, but I really hope our youth will think more actively about these issues and choose their own path.

Summary

- Fully implement IT solutions in government to reduce the number of public employees by half, and work to reform the high-cost government structure.
- Set a KPI stating that the annual cost of government services should not exceed 20 percent of the GDP, and reduce administrative expenses.

- Eliminate regional monopolies in power production, and lower the cost of electricity.
- Do away with the belief that subsidies are always the answer, and create tax credits for investments in R&D.
- Introduce a system to make the director and vice minister positions of ministries and government agencies into political appointments.
- Place greater value on the role of the Council on Economic and Fiscal Policy as a government think tank, appoint leaders to it from the private sector, and expand its powers.

5

The Power to Succeed Overseas

The Decline in the Number of Students Studying Abroad

Hiroshi: I want to discuss measures for global expansion and management capability. While I initially thought that the overseas sales of Japanese corporations were high, I found them to be surprisingly low when actually looking at the statistics. Sales peaked in 2007 at 13 percent of total sales, while they were just 11.7 percent in 2010, according to data from that year. We have gone from simpler times in which products were made entirely in Japan and then exported to a period of globalization in which production is stretched across different borders. At the same time, the use of English has become a primary factor in global business success. The movement that began when I established English as our corporate language is starting to spread and take hold.

That said, as of 2010, Japan's average TOEFL score was just 70 points out of 120—fourth from the bottom in Asia, just before Laos. South Korea sent more than 72,000 exchange students to the United States that year. Japan, in comparison, sent just under 20,000—a dramatic difference. Looking at all destinations, including the United States, the total number of students going abroad peaked in 2004 at more than 80,000. This number fell to 60,000 by 2009, and it continues to fall today. Based on this data, it seems like Japanese students are becoming increasingly inward-looking. We must do something about this situation.

One of the many obstacles to globalization and encouraging students to travel abroad is the fact that large corporations don't seem to value personnel with international experience. Japan has made the decision to participate in negotiations for the Trans-Pacific Partnership, but we continue to debate which fields should be outside the scope of compromise. From an economic perspective, I think it would be a bit of a travesty to sacrifice the automotive industry and save agriculture.

Ryoichi: Sacrificing the automotive industry isn't an option.

Hiroshi: We should have been working toward market liberalization from the very beginning. Of course we need to make exceptions for things that threaten the security of the state, but I think we should make progress toward globalization on all matters related to corporate governance, including international accounting standards. And from there we should construct a system to create frameworks that could draw the world's top business leaders to Japan. In order to do that, we need to increase the pay of business leaders in Japan. Japanese business leaders don't get paid enough.

If the current situation continues, even those who have the skill to lead businesses will be reluctant to take on that responsibility. This relates to why there is so little progress in the elimination and consolidation of businesses in the market. When businesses merge, business leaders here tend to be demoted, and so they try to avoid business elimination and consolidation because it means personal loss. Conversely, in the United States, there is the term "golden parachute," which refers to the fairly large rewards leaders receive after a merger.

Another issue that I think is important is stock compensation plans. At Rakuten, executive-level personnel receive 30 percent of their bonuses in stock. Many of the IT and financial companies in the United States have adopted this kind of stock compensation plan, because it helps maintain an entrepreneurial culture among their leaders. I have heard that some of the companies I compete with pay out any remuneration exceeding U.S. $130,000—or approximately 13 million yen—entirely in stock. What this means is that someone earning 100 million yen per year would receive just 13 million yen in cash and the remaining 87 million yen in stock. In doing so, companies can align the interests of their leaders with the company's success.

Ryoichi: It's unique that you pay out bonuses in stock.

Hiroshi: We really struggled to introduce a stock compensation plan at Rakuten. The current legal system makes it difficult for Japanese companies to use this sort of plan.

Ryoichi: You don't need to use a stock compensation plan. It may be better to create a different sort of incentive system—just as long as it motivates business leaders.

Hiroshi: There are far fewer business schools in Japan compared to Europe or the United States. It's a serious problem. We are also far behind the rest of the world in IT education. There are just 20,000 Japanese people who graduate with degrees related to computer science or programming each year. In the United States, that figure is at least over 60,000 people, and much more in India and China. Some might say that we need to compete on quality, not quantity, but with one-third the number of IT professionals as they have in the United States, I think we are facing a critical situation.

At Rakuten, we are now testing out an initiative to make programming our next common corporate language after English, although we remain at an impasse in terms of English usage. I touched on this topic earlier, but there are in fact many people who have not achieved a practical command of English, even though they have good TOEIC scores. Our next immediate goal is to address that issue.

One reason why Japanese people don't study abroad is that, in doing so, they miss out on opportunities to look for work here. The second reason is the lack of funding for studies abroad. The third is that it is too comfortable to continue living in Japan, and this has created a kind of moratorium. To be sure, things are changing at corporations. We are seeing some progress to address the impression that studying abroad can harm a student's ability to find a job. I think we are going to see dramatic change in the study-abroad situation over the next few years.

Ryoichi: If there is no negative impact in terms of their job search for people who don't go abroad, students won't go. The point is whether corporations are giving preference to people with study-abroad experience or English skills and how they differentiate those candidates from other students.

Hiroshi: Definitely.

Ryoichi: Another thing is how we recognize the ability to speak English. I am not talking about test scores or certificates; I mean the ability to actually use English. I think it's fine if people can only speak broken English, but what is important is that we evaluate their ability to find new customers and conduct business negotiations. I think people need to have a high level of English to understand delicate nuances in conversation, but in reality, business conversation tends to be limited to phrases like: "How much? That's too expensive. Make it cheaper." [laughs]

Hiroshi: When you have an evaluation framework like the one traditionally used in Japan in which we offer promotions based on seniority, there is little connection between the ways workers are evaluated and whether they have experience studying abroad or hold a master of business administration (MBA) degree or any sort of special qualifications. I would say that the return on the investment in gaining such experience is low. At Rakuten, we don't take that approach. If people are skilled, it doesn't matter if they are still in their twenties, we will select them for management positions and place them at the top of a business division. As long as people are skilled, regardless of whether they graduated from a business school and got an MBA, we have a framework in place that will allow them to move up in the company very quickly. At most Japanese companies, even if they do send people abroad to get an MBA, they tend to assign those people to domestic operations after they get back. [laughs]

Even though a company made the effort to send people to a business school abroad, in the end it becomes just another tool to hire more people. They just want to be able to say: "If you come work for us, you'll have the opportunity to go abroad." But in actuality, a lot of the

people who are sent abroad quit after they are called back
to Japan, even at the largest companies. [laughs]

Ryoichi: Why is that, I wonder? You quit your job at the
Industrial Bank of Japan after they called you back as well.

Hiroshi: Companies try to attach a lot of conditions to
studies abroad, but these conditions aren't legally binding.
I quit my job at the bank two years after returning from
my studies at Harvard University, and, let me tell you,
during that time I had produced quite a bit of profit at the
bank. Even after quitting, I still felt a certain amount of
obligation to them, which is why Mizuho Bank, the
current incarnation of the Industrial Bank of Japan, is
Rakuten's corporate bank. I think they made a pretty
penny off me in the end! [laughs]

Escaping from the Galapagos Effect

Hiroshi: In terms of macroeconomics, without a fluid
workforce, industry as a whole will not grow. Yet, when
we look at an industry, we don't see companies making an
effort to adopt international standards. I worry that the
Ministry of Economy, Trade and Industry (METI) may be
intentionally working to create this kind of industrial
structure. The main initiatives needed in order to
encourage workforce fluidity are the elimination of
Galapagos-esque regulations in the communications and
medical industries and the creation of an environment
to foster global expansion capabilities among the
corporations of Japan.

Ryoichi: What do you mean by Galapagos-esque regulations
in the medical industry?

Hiroshi: For example, the digitization of data—not being
able to digitize patient records—as well as regulations

related to doctor licensing. Say that doctors with a medical license from Japan move to the United States. They can participate in clinical research and if they pass the national test, they can be licensed to practice medicine there [although they would need an immigration visa (permanent residence) in order to open a practice]. However, if foreign doctors move to Japan, unless they start over and get licensed through the Japanese system, they are greatly limited in the extent that they can practice medicine. Standards governing medical treatments, medications, and medical devices are also suffering this Galapagos effect. A vivid example of this is the next-generation network (NGN) being advanced by NTT.

Ryoichi: I'm not very familiar with the NGN. What does it mean?

Hiroshi: The Internet should basically allow open communication. I mean, everything is done on the Internet. Yet, the NGN places a number of controls on the Internet itself.

Ryoichi: Really? I haven't heard anything about it.

Hiroshi: China is controlling access via the Internet to other countries. They are doing so using Japanese technology that alters IP addresses. The NGN is similar; although there is supposedly a prohibition on transferring IP addresses, the NGN does just that. In other words, through the NGN, they are trying to build a non–Internet network on the Internet. Both routers and servers are forced to comply with the NGN, creating a specialized structure that is only used in Japan. Doing things like this really increases costs.

One might say that this doesn't matter because it will enable NTT Group manufacturers and major IT companies to continue to make money. But because this is

not being done anywhere else in the world, it's creating a
Galapagos effect. And for that reason, at the Industrial
Competiveness Council, I strongly called for the opening
of the NGN.

Galapagos-esque regulations that protect the communications and broadcasting industry are already producing
terrible consequences. Through the creation of these
nontariff barriers, we have seen the advancement of
domestic policies that can only be applied to Japan.
Connectivity restrictions on mobile phones ended in huge
losses when smartphones were introduced, for instance.

Ryoichi: And as a result, it is more difficult for foreign
companies to enter our market.

Hiroshi: It isn't just that. These things cause Japanese
companies to lose their global competitiveness. In order
to establish global expansion and management capability,
it is important to secure an open market and introduce the
principle of competition into the way businesses are run.
In other words, we must globalize governance.

To that end, we should make overly protective
measures that prevent Japanese companies from
completing corporate takeovers illegal. I would take it
even further to say that it would be fine if unprofitable
Japanese companies were bought by foreign firms.
Because if they are bought, it doesn't matter as long as
they return to profit. Japanese companies are purchasing
companies overseas, and we need to make this a fair
system. For example, in the case of Sharp, I think it would
have been great if they had been bought by Foxconn [Hon
Hai Precision Industry Co., Ltd., a Taiwanese company]
or Samsung. And that could have happened. But then that
whole affair with their Sakai Display Product [the former
Sakai Plant] making liquid crystal displays for Sharp ended

with Foxconn merely making an investment, and not a single person at the plant was fired. In just one month, the investment brought the plant back from the brink.

Ryoichi: There is a lot here I don't know about. [laughs] From the perspective of my generation, I've been familiar with Sharp ever since their mechanical pencils were such a big hit. They are a good company. Everyone uses Sharp products. I can only think that a lot of the responsibility for them being allowed to drift toward such a poor position without anyone stepping in and doing something about it lies with the management. They needed to aggressively put something out before reaching that point. After all, a good offense is the best defense. Their founder, Tokuji Hayakawa, must be rolling over in his grave.

The Future of Journalism

Hiroshi: In this same vein, I think it must be said that media is vital to destroying Galapagos regulations. Journalism has a major role to play in spreading information to a wider audience.

Ryoichi: I agree. What's happening with journalism in Japan right now?

Hiroshi: Domestic Galapagos conditions are best for bureaucrats who are trying to control industry. By establishing such conditions, they can eliminate foreign investment. You see, because they can't control foreign investments, they create a system that can eliminate them. In order to do so, they must first brainwash the Japanese public. So they don't promote English education. And to control the media, they create press clubs. That might sound crazy, but this is what's happening.

Ryoichi: Back when I was researching monetary policy, the Bank of Japan and Ministry of Finance also had their own press clubs. I wonder if this system is unique to Japan?

Hiroshi: Journalism has the function of communicating facts and plays the role of analyzing those facts. I think the significance of that communicative function is being challenged by the spread of the Internet. And I think the press club system is working to stubbornly beat back that challenge and protect the old ways. This may be the source of what is going wrong in Japan. I think we need to destroy this system as soon as we possibly can.

Ryoichi: When I was a student, the newspaper reporters were held in the highest regard—the kind of profession that people dreamed of. I wonder what young people think these days.

Hiroshi: Just looking at the data, reporters' popularity has fallen, as have applications to join. Rather than dreaming of pursuing journalism as a profession, I think a lot of students want to join companies because the work is more stable, or they want to join newspapers or television stations because the pay is higher.

When the Internet was first getting popular, I originally thought that it would cause a massive leap in progress for journalism. I thought that newspapers could become paperless and there would no longer be problems with television frequency range. But as business started to dry up, I think journalists started to trend toward more paparazzilike special reports—more sensational news.

But then when the Abe administration took power in 2012, I felt the mood shift a little once again. Along with the great change in politics, the economy, and society, I think the number of articles that attempted to get to the bottom of Japan's issues increased. It is especially in times like these that journalists must confront politicians and bureaucrats. Journalists must not simply communicate what the government organizations are saying, but they must also take a global perspective and write in-depth articles.

The state of Japanese media, with its prefectural license system for broadcasters and press club system for journalists, allows the government and bureaucracy to collude toward the control of journalism. We have an extremely outdated framework. That we have not yet overcome that level of journalism even in the era of the Internet is a huge problem.

Ryoichi: One of my close friends when I was studying abroad at Harvard was a man named Dinsdale. He later became a professor at Queen's College at Oxford University in the United Kingdom, and I visited him many times while he was there. I remember asking him once where he thought students at Oxford most wanted to work after graduating. "They want to be journalists, of course," he said. It left a big impression on me. He believed that more than businesspeople or managers at major corporations, the students of Oxford wanted to be journalists. The social position of opinion leaders was extremely high at that time. He even considered becoming a journalist himself instead of staying at the university to do research. That was how it was among the elites of the United Kingdom back then.

All of this is to say that I think it's a problem if the Japanese students aiming to be journalists are choosing newspapers or television stations because the pay is good or the work is stable. Now that I think about it, it actually seems like journalists are becoming more like businesspeople. The issue here is, why is that happening? Why is it that the people choosing to become journalists in the United States and United Kingdom are becoming opinion leaders, while Japanese journalists are becoming businesspeople? What is the source of that qualitative difference?

Hiroshi: Basically, I think this is the same lifetime employment issue that we discussed earlier [Chapter 2]. People who go to *Yomiuri Shimbun* stay there over their entire careers—they never move to *Asahi Shimbun* or anything like that.[1] And that being the case, employees end up writing their articles in such a way that their opinions come to run along the same lines as those of the editor-in-chief or the editorial board of the paper they're at.

Ryoichi: From the very beginning, newspapers in the United States have been opinion papers. Americans really care about what opinions are written in the newspaper, such as the editorial section of the *New York Times*. Why don't Japanese newspapers debate or fight over opinions?

Hiroshi: Basically, they write only in their editorials.

Ryoichi: The editorials, yes.

Hiroshi: The government and media in Japan are connected at many levels. Politicians interfere in mass media reporting, and the more influential journalists interfere in politics. Times are greatly changing, but none of them have realized yet that there is anything wrong with the way they're acting. That's one of the reasons why I am so excited to see how politics will change with the shift to allow campaigning on the Internet.

Ryoichi: What will change the most as a result of the end of the prohibition against Internet campaigning?

Hiroshi: I think we will see an increase in voter turnout. I don't know if this is going to happen during the very first election after this change, but I do think that more young people will vote. A similar change in South Korea caused

---

[1]Both *Yomiuri Shimbun* and *Asahi Shimbun* are major Japanese newspapers.

voter turnout to rise by up to 20 percent. Once more young people start to vote, even more middle-aged and elderly people will go to vote as well—the overall interest in politics will increase. And people will stop blindly believing whatever journalists and the media say.

The most significant gap between Western media and the media of Japan comes in covering issues with a global perspective. Looking at the media in Europe and the United States, even among economics articles, people are introducing and debating not just the reality and trials of their own country, but also those of everywhere else in the world. They are even analyzing the Abenomics being implemented in Japan from a global perspective. They are debating whether the huge investment being made will really be effective. The media of Japan, by contrast, is debating Japanese policies in extremely trivial terms. Few articles examine the issues as deeply as they would be examined in the media of Europe or the United States.

Ryoichi: Reading the newspapers here, I think the level of coverage doesn't extend too far beyond a report of which Liberal Democratic Party of Japan faction leader or group chairman said what.

Media in the Internet Era

Ryoichi: Among magazines, too, I feel like there were much better debates taking place in general monthly magazines like *Bungei Shunju* and *Chuo Koron* in the past.

Hiroshi: That sort of media should work to develop wider readership again via the Internet. E-publishing can mitigate the costs of printing and binding and eliminate issues like inventory risk. Magazines should lower costs accordingly and work to increase readership. I think the cultural standards of Japan would increase if they did.

It's too bad that this sort of thing isn't being done today. Any way you look at it, magazines should use e-publishing. Yet some firms are charging more for digital distribution than for paper copies.

Ryoichi: The elimination of inventory costs is huge. It's essential that they digitize.

Hiroshi: I think they should lower prices in accordance with the lowered costs. In any case, the important issue here is how journalists use Internet media. Another thing that I want to mention is the need to change the business model of the media.

Ryoichi: How can the media survive in the Internet era?

Hiroshi: By promoting digitization, producing content with actual value, and setting appropriate pricing. I think the best media company right now may just be the general information service company Bloomberg in the United States. Bloomberg is not just publishing straight news, but they are also creating rich content. And they do not just publish news on the Internet; they also work with traditional television broadcasting, radio stations, and satellite broadcasters. Furthermore, not only do they operate multiple media outlets, but they also lower costs through innovative methods such as having one-person film crews covering news stories.

Ryoichi: They are doing filming with just one person?

Hiroshi: Yes, they are extremely efficient in the way they are doing television recordings. I would estimate that they are keeping costs at about one-third the price of what it costs for a Japanese company to do it. They also have rules related to how many articles a journalist publishes per week and how many awards those articles win, and if journalists don't meet their quotas, they are fired. These are key performance indicators (KPIs) to the letter. And whether that is a good idea or not, the fact of the matter is that their business is growing. One reason for that, to use an older term, is that they *diversify* the media they are involved in. They also prioritize the depth of coverage over how recent the news is, and they specialize in explaining what the news means.

In June 2013, the Japan Association of New Economy held a forum entitled "Questioning Abenomics," to which we invited guests such as Eiji Ogawa, Vice President of Hitotsubashi University, and Heizo Takenaka, Professor at Keio University. Hosting this kind of forum is something that people in the media should be doing, but because they aren't, we are. Although I did wonder at the time, "Wait, why is this our job?" [laughs]

Ryoichi: I think journalism is really important. My belief is that, from the perspective of improving Japanese society as a whole, journalists must have their own, independent opinions. And to that end, I think journalists must all function as researchers in the widest sense of that word.

Hiroshi: Yes, but in Japan, we still think of newspaper journalists as *paper men*.

Ryoichi: That particular term communicates a contempt of journalism. Journalists have a responsibility to interact with researchers, develop their own opinions, and communicate those opinions to society. What I cannot understand is why we are not fostering journalists with their own opinions in Japan.

Hiroshi: I think that is because the editorial departments in newspapers aren't independent of the management departments.

Ryoichi: No, they aren't.

Hiroshi: The structure at newspapers is one in which reporters work their way up toward becoming the head of the paper. There is a culture among reporters of going along with their bosses. In the United States, people often talk about Rupert Murdoch as the king of media, but when he bought the *Wall Street Journal*, the paper devoted its front page to the story and offered very objective and calm commentary on the acquisition. When Rakuten tried to buy TBS, it was a different story altogether. [laughs] Not only TBS, but all of the other print and broadcasting media outlets criticized us, too.

Ryoichi: They did. You received a lot of heat. What happened there? Why didn't that work out better?

Hiroshi: My perspective now is that it was a lost cause from the start. The business model of broadcasting is tied to the monopolization of broadcasting signals. It involves a huge privilege. Whoever tries to get in on that will be pushed out of the market. This isn't a nice way of putting it, but having a destroyer like me [laughs] enter the industry is a problem not just for TBS, but perhaps even for the industry as a whole.

In the United States, however, whether you look at Bloomberg or a general media company like Time Warner, each company is always trying to find innovative ways to reach its respective audiences. By getting more involved in different types of media, they are delving deeper into a wider range of content. The strength of their management teams is crucial as they pursue these efforts. They need to consider how to price content, how to create a framework that can make that content profitable, and what sort of business models to construct. With some deep thinking, they can enhance sales a great deal. But in the unpredictable situation faced in Japan right now, I don't think there are any leaders in the mass media who are exercising good management capabilities.

Ryoichi: It's hard for me to think that there are good management capabilities among the mass media companies of Japan. Being a good journalist and managing the company are totally different jobs. Each requires very unique skills and talent.

Hiroshi: We are seeing a kind of tectonic shift in the broadcasting industry here, but because the old ways of doing things are also still being practiced, the industry is sinking deeper and deeper into a quagmire.

Ryoichi: Like NHK[2] here in Japan, the United Kingdom also has a public broadcasting corporation, the British Broadcasting Corporation. NHK is a special case in the Japanese media industry, but how does it stack up? After all, NHK doesn't just carry news programs, it also broadcasts a lot of entertainment programming.

Hiroshi: I think everyone has wondered at some point why NHK is showing the U.S. Major League Baseball games. [laughs] It's nonsense. [laughs] One thing about NHK, though, is that they do criticize the government a surprising amount.

Ryoichi: I would think that is because the worst possible situation for them would be to be accused of being a puppet of the government. Above all else, neutrality is very important for them. After all, in NHK's case, they are responsible to everyone in the public, because everyone is required to pay broadcasting fees by law, although I know there are a lot of people who don't pay.

Hiroshi: I think an issue here is whether we really need NHK. I also think it is crucial that we auction licenses for space in the broadcasting spectrum. Along with progress in technology that can do data conversions, we should be able to carry a great many more channels within the current spectrum. Then again, we continue to see a Galapagos situation by which the number of channels is

---

[2]NHK (abbreviation of Nippon Hoso Kyokai, or Japan Broadcasting Corporation in English) is Japan's publicly owned broadcasting corporation funded by viewers' payments of a television license fee.

being reduced through advancements in high–definition broadcasting.

Ryoichi: By suppressing the number of available channels, television companies are protecting their monopolies.

Hiroshi: It's just the same as the convoy system; it's all being advanced by bureaucrats. Those same bureaucrats are quitting their jobs in government for cushy jobs in media. The fates of television companies are tied to the METI and the Ministry of Internal Affairs and Communications. And the companies are doing everything they can to prevent people from watching television on the Internet. As discussed earlier [Chapter 4], they are trying just as hard to prevent commercials for smart TVs from being broadcast on television.

Ryoichi: Is it possible to watch television over the Internet right now?

Hiroshi: Because Internet is connected to television, I think it will only be two or three years before that's possible. Times will then be quite tough for television stations.

To be honest, at that point I think we will see the emergence of real journalism. We are seeing very primitive forays into journalism already on popular video–streaming sites niconico, YouTube, and Ustream. Regardless of whether the niconico format is the best option, it's definitely interesting to watch because it's interactive. I just think that the content being broadcast by those journalists isn't very good yet. The journalists on the site right now are nothing more than discussion facilitators who lack the discretion to steer the conversation. But that being the case, if they don't at least organize the differing views and submit them to the public for consideration, there can be no debate at a national level.

Ryoichi: Every newspaper is saying the exact same things about Abenomics.

Hiroshi: High-level journalism does not spread populism. There is a need for it to continuously publish critical reporting. To that end, there is a need to separate journalism from politicians, the bureaucracy, and government officials, and journalists must write their articles from a position of having pride in their profession.

The Importance of Liberal Arts

Ryoichi: I was surprised to hear the statistic that the number of Japanese students studying abroad fell by half in the five years following the peak year of 2004. I'm concerned that this will become a long-term trend.

Hiroshi: I think we need to change the reality of the situation, which is that students don't feel any need to go out of their way to study abroad.

Ryoichi: We need to change the way that young people think, but I also wonder if a cause of concern here isn't the high cost of university education in the United States compared to Japan?

Hiroshi: State universities aren't that expensive. It's the famous private schools like Harvard and Stanford that are still really pricey. The thing is, tuition at these pricey universities is set according to the income of the student's parents and the potential of the student.

In the United States, tuition levels based on students' ability to fund their own education still make it much cheaper than universities in Japan. I think the good points about Japanese universities are that the average tuition is cheap and the universities are fair.

Hiroshi: I visited Harvard the other day and spoke to some professors there and noticed that each of the famous schools of the United States prioritize liberal arts. But Japan seems to be shifting toward more specialized education and training. What do you think about that?

Ryoichi: It's definitely true that universities in the United States prioritize a liberal arts education that fosters their students' humanity. Specialized education usually starts from around the second half of the student's third year. Then again, at Harvard Medical School, courses split and move toward specialization from the beginning of the third year onward.

Hiroshi: I think the medical field is a special case, because the students choose their specialization. For other fields, specialized education basically means graduate school.

Ryoichi: That's why there is Harvard College and separate graduate schools, such as the medical school and business school.

Hiroshi: I think specialized education is important, but I also feel we place too little emphasis on liberal arts in Japan. I mean, how do you even say "liberal arts" in Japanese?

Ryoichi: "General education."

Hiroshi: Put simply, it's an education that teaches students how to think. By learning about historic events and philosophies, students can analyze the events and affairs of the world and gain the capacity to really think for themselves. I wonder if that concept is something that just isn't a part of Japanese culture?

Ryoichi: There used to be liberal arts faculties at the national universities of Japan. These days the only remnant of those programs is at the University of Tokyo, and they are in the process of getting rid of it. Students here test into universities with their faculty and degree already decided. I wonder if we aren't asking people to choose their specialization too early. And another thing: This is just my impression, but the people of the United States and United Kingdom seem to express their opinions clearly in speech, and they also place a very high priority on being able to write. In Japan, students do this in their Japanese class or if they have to write a short paper, but I really think there are very few chances for them to summarize and express their own opinions.

In fact, you know when I was at Harvard, the thing that I really had the hardest time with was writing out my own thoughts on something in an essay. It used to take me hours. My classmates would finish their assignments without any problems. How was it when you studied abroad?

Hiroshi: Well, let's just say that English isn't an easy language! [laughs]

Ryoichi: How about your papers?

Hiroshi: Because I'm a businessperson, I can make do with the bare minimum. [laughs]

Ryoichi: But I'm sure you had to write essays in business school.

Hiroshi: Basically all of the tests used an essay format. Theories of education in Japan are really just about memorizing the knowledge, which is to say that I don't feel like they are really used at all. For instance, ask a bureaucrat at the Ministry of Education, Culture, Sports, Science and Technology about theories or methodology of English education, and they can't even answer the question. [laughs] There are many different ways to approach methods of learning language, including theories and approaches that closely connect to neurology, but it feels like people aren't even considering these basic concepts. Now, there might be a specialized division

within the ministry, I don't know, but I can at least say
that my questions flustered a bureaucrat who is supposed
to be in charge of English education. I strongly feel that
we must think about education in more strategic ways.

Ryoichi Mikitani's Experiences Abroad

Hiroshi: You mastered English in your teens and undertook
the challenge of going abroad to the United States right
after World War II, at a time when travel abroad was a rare
thing. What first made you want to study English?

Ryoichi: I was 15 years old right after the end of the war in
the summer of 1945 when the occupying forces came to
Kobe. They set up their headquarters in the Daimaru
Department Store building and built housing for the
officers around Kobe University. During the war, we
talked about the Americans and British as being demons
and beasts, so I was surprised to see how normal they
were when I actually met American soldiers. [laughs]
I remember one day when a black soldier came to the
well asking for water. And I remember him saying that
there was no water as delicious as what we gave him there.

Hiroshi: You've mentioned your water problem to me a lot.

Ryoichi: Right. The way I pronounced "water" sounded
to the Americans like I was saying "wo-u-ta-a." My
pronunciation was entirely wrong. That was a shock.
I remember thinking that I needed to study English more,
so I started going to the Palmore Institute at night—it's a
school set up by missionaries. I studied English from
native speakers there. That was also when I was in the
preparatory course for Kobe University of Economics,
before it became Kobe University.

Hiroshi: You also studied German.

Ryoichi: I took German as a second language while taking preparatory courses to enter a university. In the beginning, I thought I would go to Germany, so I took classes at the Goethe-Institut, which was built while I was in the university in Kobe. I even received a letter of recommendation from them and was just about to decide to study abroad in Germany when I saw an article about Fulbright scholarships in a newspaper.

The Fulbright scholarships are the result of a proposal by the U.S. senator J. William Fulbright in an effort to deepen mutual understanding among the United States and other regions of the world. The program is run here by the Japan–U.S. Educational Commission [Fulbright Japan], which is funded by both the Japanese and U.S. governments, and it has offered financial support to students doing specialized research through studies abroad since 1952. I took the test without putting too much thought into it, and I somehow passed the interview that took place there.

Hiroshi: That's how you studied abroad at Harvard.

Ryoichi: I studied abroad as a matriculated student at Harvard University in the city of Cambridge, Massachusetts, in the United States as a Fulbright exchange student. I became an assistant professor at Kobe University of Commerce at the age of 29 in 1959. That was a time when it was difficult to know about what was going on overseas without studying abroad, and so I wanted to study the latest economic research from the United States, not just for the purpose of advancing my own work, but also so I could pass that knowledge on to my colleagues and students. I flew on a propeller plane to get there. I first flew to Hawaii and then flew to San Francisco.

Hiroshi: What was your first impression upon arriving at San Francisco?

Ryoichi: It's a terrible thing, but I came down with
hemorrhoids right before leaving Japan. [laughs] So I
went to a clinic in San Francisco and got some antibiotics,
which I used with warm water to cure my problem.
I remember being shocked at how different medicine
was in the United States compared to Japan.

I crossed the United States from the west coast to the
east coast on a locomotive. I was traveling by myself, and
there were no other Japanese people on the train. I didn't
feel any discrimination then, and I remember thinking
how nice it was that people in the United States were
so frank.

There was an orientation program in Colorado for
Fulbright exchange students. There were about 10
Japanese students there, and about half of them were
university teachers like me. Yoshiro Tamanoi, the Marxist
economist from the University of Tokyo, was among
them. And then there were bankers.

Hiroshi: You could communicate in English.

Ryoichi: I had studied at the Palmore Institute, so I didn't
have any trouble with conversations or the kind of English
used in university courses. I had U.S. $230 a month to
live off, which is about U.S. $2,000 in today's money.
I stayed at a place near the university.

While I was at Harvard, I took monetary theory from
Duesenberry and Hendrik Samuel Houthakker, and I also
took economic theory from Robert Dorfman. Among
the professors were also people like Wassily Leontief,
a Jewish man who had fled for his life from Germany.
Leontief won a Nobel Prize in Economics in 1973, and
I remember wondering why such an amazing academic
would pursue economics. Seeing the way he connected
the different real issues in economics and thought about
them was inspiring.

Hiroshi: Were your studies difficult?

Ryoichi: My schedule was full from Monday to Friday. I remember always thinking that I had to take this test or write that paper, but it was satisfying. I spent a year at Harvard and then another year at Stanford University in California thanks to a scholarship I received from the Japan Society, a nonprofit organization that works to spread Japanese culture in the United States. I spent a total of more than two years studying abroad in the United States from my start in June 1959 until September 1961. I married Setsuko in 1956, and we lived together for that second year in Silicon Valley. We lived in a house owned by the Concannon Vineyard. We lived under one roof and got along well with the Concannon family. We still do today.

The second time I studied abroad lasted for just over two years from July 1972 until September 1974, while I was a professor at Kobe University. I received a scholarship from the American Comparative Literature Association, and I used it to work as a visiting fellow at Yale University in New Haven, Connecticut. We all moved there together. You were in your second year of elementary school.

Summary

- Introduce a stock-option reward system in the private sector.
- Set a KPI calling for an increase in the number of students studying abroad by the tens of thousands.
- Promote English as the second language of Japan and as the language of business.
- Eliminate the prefectural broadcasting license and press club systems.

6

The Power to Educate

Uniform Japanese Education

Hiroshi: Let's talk now about the problems facing education. I have the feeling that the thinking about education has been different in the United States and Japan from the very beginning. What do you think?

Ryoichi: In Japan's case, education has literally been about teaching and fostering knowledge. In the United States, it has been all about education—in other words, "to educe" (to bring out potential). That's the etymology of the word, and it exemplifies how education in the United States is concerned with drawing out the abilities of those being taught. In that sense, the concept of education differs between Japan and the United States. Education in Japan is influenced by Confucius. I believe that in China they have the same feelings as we do.

In the United States, students start asking more
questions from an early age, but in Japan, we teach through
a top-down educational structure. I went to observe one
of your classes when you were in elementary school, and
I remember seeing that for myself. That same principle of
teaching and fostering by the teacher is prevalent in Japan's
universities as well.

Hiroshi: I feel that in Japan, and in elementary and junior
high school in particular, education is extremely uniform
and based on receiving and following instructions. My
strong feeling is that this is a framework designed to
produce robotlike students. There are those in politics and
finance who have even said that Japanese young people
are a lost cause and that we need to reintroduce the draft
to fix that. But military organizations are truly based on a
structure of receiving instructions and acting upon them.
What's more, I have heard neurologists say that forcing
children to follow orders during puberty, when their
brains are really still growing, is the worst thing we can do
to them. Asking people to obey your instructions is the
same as telling them not to think.

Ryoichi: It really does mean telling people to stop thinking.

Hiroshi: We need to balance thinking capabilities with the
capacity to follow rules, but I can't help but think we are
leaning too far toward instruction following in Japanese
education. And in any case, I never followed the rules as a
child, did I? [laughs] And I certainly didn't ever listen to
you and mom. [laughs]

Ryoichi: You didn't listen to your teachers, either.

Hiroshi: Well, there was no way I was going to listen to my
teachers. [laughs] I was the kind of child who wanted to
break the mold from the very beginning, so I was going
to have doubts about fitting into that mold. I feel like

there is no room for creativity or free thought in an education system based on following orders.

Ryoichi: I agree.

Hiroshi: We are no longer in an era in which we need a uniform education system to create blue-collar workers for factories. At Rakuten we have a genius engineer who earned a PhD at Harvard, and I remember very well something he said to me: Rules are something people learn so that they can understand the most efficient ways to achieve their goals. The use of equations is a good example of this. It's something that is done so that you don't have to consider unnecessary things as you solve the problem at hand. The rules are there so you don't have to think.

Ryoichi: It is about economization—reducing wasteful actions.

Hiroshi: Yes, but what is important here is that people shouldn't just follow the rules blindly. They should follow the rules knowing how and why those rules were made. So, they should know why we don't cross the street at a red light, for instance. I feel that education in Japan is missing that part of the equation.

The Education of the Mikitani Family

Hiroshi: What was your approach to raising kids?

Ryoichi: I never wanted a home where the parents would simply instruct their children, commanding them to study and so forth. I recognized that each child has his or her own character, and I tried to teach without holding to any set pattern. Probably just about the only lessons that I ever really tried to drill into your heads were things like don't steal, tell the truth, and don't bully those weaker than you.

Hiroshi: Definitely. It was a very free home environment.

Ryoichi: Even though you were born in March, you were big for your age, and you had a knack for anything physical.[1] Right when most kids were finally riding a tricycle, you were already riding a bike. [laughs]

I was a professor at the Kobe University of Commerce around that time, and we lived in instructor's lodging at one side of a residential area managed by the university. There were about 20 houses there. We lived alongside my coworkers and their families, so there were a lot of children your age around, and you were all friends. You always went out to play in a huge group.

Hiroshi: I remember a boy named Obayashi.

Ryoichi: He lived next door. You two rode the bus to kindergarten together. You were so social, so you were very popular in kindergarten. I even heard that you already had a girlfriend then. [laughs] But then once you went to elementary school, you wouldn't listen to your teachers. You had to go stand in the corner a lot.

Hiroshi: I think I remember there being 10 classes of first graders that year and there not being enough classrooms, so we had to go learn in a prefab building.

Ryoichi: That did happen, didn't it? Ikuko [Hiroshi's older sister] was a sixth grader then, and her class was on the building's fourth floor. Her classmates apparently used to tease her by letting her know every time you were made to stand in the corner. [laughs]

Hiroshi: Well, I don't remember anything about that. [laughs] I suppose they made me stand because I didn't retain what I learned. [laughs]

Ryoichi: You didn't do your homework. There were other things, too, but that's the kind of stuff that your teachers

---

[1] In Japan, children start their primary schooling at different ages. Since primary schools accept entering students only once a year in April, those who are born in April are more mature in their grade than those who are born in March, in terms of their physical and mental development.

got angry about. I heard that one of your teachers threw chalk at you once. Was that true?

Hiroshi: I remember catching the chalk in my hat. [laughs]

Ryoichi: In spite of all of that, you certainly played a lot. You were a regular genius when it came to goofing off. [laughs] But you weren't a mean kid, you were quite sweet.

Hiroshi: I played baseball outdoors, games like Kick the Can. I was always with my friends. I would bring them home or go over to their houses.

Ryoichi: There were times that we worried because you hadn't come back until past eight. We would take drives in our new car on the weekend, and I remember that we even went to Mount Rokko and amusement parks together as a family.

When I was studying abroad at Yale in the United States you would have been in the autumn of your second year of elementary school. We went as a family of five to the United States and spent over two years there. There were 20 people in your elementary school class in the United States, and I recall your teacher being very kind.

Hiroshi: I remember bringing friends home the very first day that we moved to the United States. I was good at making friends, so it was fun. In the beginning I only knew how to say "one, two, three" and some other things, but by the time we went back to Japan, my English was better than my Japanese.

Ryoichi: They didn't have school lunches there, so I remember you taking a lunchbox to school and eating in the cafeteria. They also didn't make you clean your classrooms like students do in Japan. And your school was very strict about security, making sure that you didn't play in the schoolyard during recess by having teachers watch you guys to make sure you didn't go outside. But the teaching style didn't involve rote memorization like it does in Japan.

Hiroshi: I'm the type of person who won't want to do something anymore if I'm told I have to do it. I won't want to do it and I won't do it. [laughs]

Ryoichi: I wonder if that's why you quit going to Okayama Hakuryo Junior High School?

Hiroshi: It's a very good school now, but back then it was a harsh environment to study in. The principal hit me a lot. The judo teacher hit me with bamboo swords and rods as well.

Ryoichi: That was the school policy. The principal was an alumnus of Himeji High School, one of the former imperial high schools in Himeji. He wanted to give the children a similar education to that found in the imperial high schools. But when the students didn't listen to their teachers, he felt there was no choice but to get tough.

I also thought that it might be better to have a more liberal education, but back then it seemed like everyone else believed that a strict, militarylike education was the best way to go, so I kept my mouth shut.

Hiroshi: Hakuryo may have needed a strict education then, but it wasn't the education that I needed then.

Ryoichi: All students were required to live in dormitories. Did you at least study a little?

Hiroshi: More or less. But the method of study was entirely based on rote memorization. They basically told us to memorize everything. For example, the English test was entirely based on memorization and covered textbook lessons from cover to cover. But our textbook was from before World War II. We also had normal textbooks, but they were almost never used. If we made even a minor spelling error, we were docked five points. If we left a letter out, we were docked ten points. Tests were out of 100 points, and we were paddled once for every five points we missed under 80 points. [laughs] This is all true.

Ryoichi: That's terrible. [laughs]

Hiroshi: I was beat every time. That may have been effective for some students, but I couldn't take it.

Ryoichi: Especially because you were placed at a dorm in Okayama prefecture.

Hiroshi: Kenichi [Hiroshi's older brother] was sent to Hakuryo Junior High School in Takasago, Hyogo Prefecture. But since my grades were awful [laughs], I was forced to go to Okayama Hakuryo Junior High School in Akaiwa, Okayama Prefecture.

Ryoichi: I was shocked when you came back for your holidays and hadn't grown at all. I remember thinking that whether you were studying or not, the situation was awful. But then I couldn't say anything about it because I felt it was all up to you, and that you would say what you were going to do. But then the following morning after you had come back home, just before you were about to leave, you announced that you were quitting school. I knew it was time to act then and there, and your mother and I worked together to get you out of there. I called your teachers at Hakuryo and the principal of a public junior high school and went in my car to pick up your stuff from the dorm that very day.

Hiroshi: That was not something that I decided suddenly that morning. I had been thinking about it for some time, and I had just come to a conclusion. I transferred into a public junior high school called Asagiri Junior High School in Akashi. Now, if you ask me whether I studied more after going to public school, my answer is no! [laughs]

Ryoichi: Students who transfer into public schools from private schools tend to have excellent grades, so your teachers had really high hopes for you, you know. Boy, were they ever wrong! [laughs]

Hiroshi: No kidding. All I did every day was play tennis. But my PE grades were awful! [laughs] I was getting Cs and Bs the whole time. I got good marks on strength tests, but when they told me to step to the right in PE, I would go left [laughs], things like that.

Ryoichi: Our whole family joined a local tennis club, and I still think that's what kept you on track.

Hiroshi: That's because everyone I played tennis with was much older.

Ryoichi: All the adults at the club loved you. Back then when we talked about your friends, it was all adults from the tennis club.

What the Education System Needs

Hiroshi: When thinking about what students should be taught in schools, I think some people believe we must teach students to love their country, and others think we need a philosophical education with something like a modern version of the *Imperial Rescript on Education*. I think we need something completely different. I think there are a lot of potential traps in that kind of pedagogy that could cause people to stop thinking. Everyone is blaming the Japan Teachers' Union for the state of education in Japan. But I also think those critics are trying to create a framework that would cause children to stop thinking and make it easier for politicians and bureaucrats to control them. That kind of educational system follows this old philosophy of "the nail that sticks up should get pounded down." I wonder if the culture of Japan wasn't entirely different before World War II and after the Meiji Restoration. Or did they have a culture that told people not to challenge their superiors? Was the education that you received at your formerly imperial high school a liberal education?

Ryoichi: The education at the former imperial schools was liberal to a certain extent, although they focused on the single important goal of creating elites. Students thought and acted freely. That is why a lot of ideas came under attack, including left-wing ideas. An interesting point, perhaps, is that the education system was not one like they currently have in China, in which students are entirely restricted in what they can do. I think if we had an education system like that, Japan would not have developed the way it has. After World War II and during the period of American occupation was a time when we valued American-style freedom. I believe that pressure in schools only started to get worse after the Cold War.

But let's say that we prioritize free thought within the mandatory lessons of primary education. In such a case, what elements would you say absolutely must be taught?

Hiroshi: Right now I would say English, which is not currently taught at the elementary school level. It is included in some curriculums for fifth and sixth graders, but it is not a mandatory course. It is up to the judgment of each school principal whether to feature English education as a part of the extracurricular classes. Because it isn't a mandatory subject, I have heard that a lot of schools teach English under the category of "foreign language activities." And they only offer one class a week of that.

Ryoichi: Really? Only one class a week?

Hiroshi: In South Korea they offer English classes two to three times per week. Over there they will make English mandatory in 10 to 20 years, so they absolutely have to make English lessons an obligatory elementary school subject now. I called for this strongly in the Industrial Competitiveness Council, and I believe that we will see a shift toward a better English education from elementary school onward in Japan moving forward.

Ryoichi: In that case, we'll need more foreign teachers.

Hiroshi: In Turkey they have set aside an annual budget equivalent to 100 billion yen [U.S. $1 billion] in order to attract tens of thousands of foreign teachers.

Ryoichi: Their children will interact with foreign nationals from a young age and gain exposure to foreign languages.

Hiroshi: I don't really think it's that difficult to enhance English proficiency. In Japan, students spend as much as approximately 2,000 hours studying English during their 12 years of primary education. I believe that people could start to speak English even without increasing the number of hours studied if we just changed the way English is taught.

Ryoichi: I've heard that they dramatically overhauled the way they teach English in South Korea. If we continue on as we are, Japan will fall behind.

Hiroshi: The education system in South Korea is amazing. The English education there is particularly great.

Ryoichi: If you go to tourist spots in Tokyo or Kyoto, you can see students visiting these places on school trips, and they are speaking in English a fair bit with foreign nationals. I think Japanese children are interested in English.

Hiroshi: Another important subject is the enhancement of our IT education. Even people aiming to be lawyers or teachers or accountants are now used to typing on a keyboard. That wasn't the case in the past. In the same way, in the future, basically everyone is going to be able to do some basic programming, even if they can't do so today. And if that's the way it's going to be eventually, I think we might as well start learning to do this kind of thing right now.

We need to raise the level of IT skills among young people in Japan and shift toward the acceptance of more foreign nationals into the workforce—to the extent that we can.

Ryoichi: You talked about your experiences with rote memorization while you were at Okayama Hakuryo Junior High School. Don't you feel that rote memorization also has its merits?

Hiroshi: As the typical example of uniform education, no, I don't. But the background to rote education pedagogy is that at one time there were few teachers, so there was no choice but to implement uniform education. At pricey private schools in the United States, there is one teacher for 10 or so kids. But in Japan, even at private schools, there is only one teacher for more than 30 kids.

Ryoichi: When the class is that big, it doesn't matter if you have 30 students or 50.

Hiroshi: The United States takes a more personalized approach to education with a higher teacher to student ratio than in Japan. And at private schools, you even have places where there is one teacher for classes of just nine students.

Ryoichi: The point being that Japan is not spending enough on education.

Hiroshi: I believe that's true. Our budget for education is too small. With the emergence of the Internet, we now have a lot of new tools at our disposal. And I believe that these tools are causing a shift in the very definitions of learning and education. The Internet changed the way we shop, and, similarly, I believe that it will fundamentally change the way we learn things. It won't be like it was in the past. Because the Internet is interactive, we should see an enhancement in the way that children can take in information. The problem is that many educators don't have the mind-set to embrace the new tools.

Ryoichi: I saw something quite a while ago that left a big impression on me. It was at a reunion for people who had gone to Stanford. About 10 or so university students from Stanford came to that reunion in Kyoto, and all of us had a meeting with them. The entire time we talked, they were typing away on their computers. Now, only recently, do you see some Japanese students who are also using laptops in class. But at that time it was completely unheard of in Japan. I was really surprised. Why has Japan been so late in introducing IT?

Hiroshi: One reason for that is that the teachers could not make use of it. Another reason is a lack of imagination—people just couldn't see that the future would be like it is. When you have a uniform education, it is very rigid in the sense that it is education going in just one direction. That is why you see people stop thinking. Some people have the vague worry that people will lose the ability to think if they converse while using a computer. [laughs]

Ryoichi: Apart from the way things are taught, I wonder if we still need reading, writing, and arithmetic to be compulsory.

Hiroshi: I quit my abacus lessons midway through, you know.

Ryoichi: You use a computer now.

Hiroshi: I think we should teach reading, writing, and arithmetic only to the least extent possible.

Ryoichi: People need to learn how to gather their thoughts, and then speak or write about them.

Hiroshi: Well, I think there may be pros and cons to what I am saying. If you look at the United Kingdom, for instance, I think the policy there of prioritizing debating and thinking has failed them. It is important that people are able to express themselves, but what is really important is that people have the ability to think about what is most important to them. The Japanese bureaucracy has typically used Kasumigaseki language to trick people. I think the arguments made by bureaucrats fall apart when they are translated into English.

Ryoichi: Oh, that's absolutely true.

Hiroshi: Japanese doesn't put things into black and white; rather, it makes everything a sort of muddied color and keeps things ambiguous. And on that point, it may be that the way of thinking among Japanese children has been molded through the long history of the culture of Japan. There has been a need to have people with the ability to fix things, somehow, even if their superiors said something wrong.

I think it is crucial that people have the ability to think logically, and it is essential that people study Japanese for that reason. It is also important to follow rules. But following rules also means compliance with common knowledge, and if everyone does that, we won't see the emergence of any superstars who can defy that common knowledge. I have to believe that the people who have broken down existing frameworks and pioneered new eras so far are people who must have been poor students when they were children. [laughs] Even Thomas Edison and Albert Einstein were probably both sort of odd.

Ryoichi: That might be true. But in that sense, so are you. [laughs]

Higher Education

Hiroshi: We have already touched upon this a little, but I want to talk some more about higher education.

In particular, I want to focus on the idea that undergraduate education is a time for students to receive both a specialized and a liberal arts education. A good amount of debate goes on about specialized education, but the liberal arts side of things tends to be neglected.

Another problem we face is the evaluation system for educators. We can't have professors who go along with populism or censor themselves just to appeal to students. But that said, I think we can't just let teachers sit on their laurels and receive the benefits of lifelong employment. University organizations, too, must evolve to remain vital.

Ryoichi: You met a cram school teacher, Yuzo Murakami, while you were taking courses at Kobe Seminar in preparation for university, and suddenly your English grades improved tremendously. What was it about him that made his teaching so effective?

Hiroshi: He had a way of really grasping each student's peculiarities and latent abilities. It was like he had the power to look at a food that no one in their right mind would want to eat and know that it would actually be delicious if you just peeled away the skin. [laughs] But he was a cram school teacher, and I think that's why it was possible for him to plainly teach. I think that would have been difficult if it had been 40 students to a class.

Ryoichi: Right, the math teacher at Hyogo Prefectural Akashi Senior High School was shocked that your progress was so fast. He told me he had never had a student grasp the material like you did. [laughs]

Hiroshi: There were over 400 students at Hyogo Prefectural Akashi Senior High School. I ranked 200 on the first test. After two months, I made my way from 200th to being in the top tier, and by the end, I finished on top as number one.

Ryoichi: That's right. What was your secret? Did you receive sort of special teaching or have some special way of learning?

Hiroshi: No, I just used the standard Obunsha textbook. [laughs]

Ryoichi: You wanted to do it and you tried your best. I never told you this, but I wrote a thank-you letter to your math teacher, and he wrote back saying, "Like pouring water into parched sand, he soaked up everything I taught him and more. I am proud to have had him as a student." He was trying his best to teach you, too. [laughs] I think it was meaningful for him.

Hiroshi: I had no idea. [laughs]

Ryoichi: All of your teachers were really good.

Hiroshi: My experience tells me that, in the first place, good teaching is not about making people remember what you want to teach. It should actually be thought of as motivation management. It is about supporting the drive people have to learn.

Ryoichi: Absolutely.

Hiroshi: I don't think anything can come of having entire classrooms pronounce, "Yes, this is a pen" in unison. [laughs] To be serious, in the three years I was in high school, I don't think I learned very much. Actually, I didn't generally go to school. [laughs] I looked at my academic records earlier, and it looks like I skipped school over 30 days when I was in my third year.

Ryoichi: Because I told you you didn't have to go. I knew that you had started studying on your own, so I thought it was a waste of time to have you go sit in on classes. Where did you study?

Hiroshi: Since you told me I didn't have to go to school, I went to study in the library. Up until that point I hadn't been going to school because I was too busy goofing off, but somewhere in my second year of high school, my destination each day changed from seeing my friends to going to the library. [laughs]

What People Study in University

Hiroshi: I get the feeling that, in the past, the formerly imperial schools provided an education with an unusual focus on liberal arts.

Ryoichi: Exactly. In general education courses, people took English and one other foreign language, and studied the Grecian and Roman classics as well as history and culture. As the educated people of Japan, students had to read intellectual and educational books such as Kitaro Nishida's *An Inquiry into the Good* and Jiro Abe's *Santaro's Diary*. My generation was educated that elites were expected to learn certain things. At some point, people stopped learning that. Setsuko graduated from Kobe University after the end of the imperial education system, but she still received a liberal arts education for a year and a half after starting university.

Hiroshi: I was once asked to speak at a commencement ceremony by the dean of Hitotsubashi University. The year before me, they had invited then-CEO of Toyota and the chairman of Keidanren Hiroshi Okuda. The dean told me he wanted me to do it, and I asked him then if it was really all right if I did. He told me it was, but then the other shoe dropped; you see, he said to me, "Just don't let anyone know that you didn't study while you were a student here."

Ryoichi: That's hilarious! [laughs]

Hiroshi: So I told him, "Yeah, it's definitely my fault for not studying. But it's also the university's fault for not

offering courses that would make me want to study."
[laughs] University courses are boring. They don't inspire
learning, and people don't grasp what they are learning if
they are only half-interested in what is being taught.

Ryoichi: I take it you didn't study much economics during
university?

Hiroshi: I did, more or less. I went to a seminar two times
a week—it was the only time I showed up to class.
Hitotsubashi University really was the kind of place where
you didn't have to study. All that mattered was that you
graduated from there, and you didn't need to go to class
to do so—as they say, "Kyoto University in the west,
Hitotsubashi University in the east."

Ryoichi: You spent the whole time playing tennis.

Hiroshi: When people asked me what faculty I was in,
I would tell them that I was in the tennis club. [laughs]
If I were to talk about what exactly I did in university,
I played tennis like it was my job, and I took general
education courses. Although I think I could have used my
time in university in a better way, club activities were the
core of university life for me, so I'm glad I did what I did.

Ryoichi: You were assigned to a seminar course with
Dr. Toshiya Hanawa in the faculty of commerce and
management of Hitotsubashi University. It must have
been very difficult to finish your graduating thesis.

Hiroshi: It was tough. I wrote my thesis on the relationship
between the number of advertisements a company puts
out and the company's value.

Ryoichi: Dr. Hanawa asked you to stay at the university.

Hiroshi: He did. I was invited to pursue research there.

Ryoichi: I remember that you came back to stay at our
home in Kobe to think it over. I believe that was before
you received the offer from the Industrial Bank of Japan,
and you came not so much for advice, but to tell me what

you were going to do. I heard what you said and advised you to reconsider. You could have stayed behind in Dr. Hanawa's seminar and become a researcher, but I think you were more suited to working at a company. And put in grander terms, that was a better choice for Japan.

Hiroshi: What sort of places did the students in your seminar at Kobe University go to work at?

Ryoichi: I had about 20 students in my seminar every year while I was a professor in the faculty of economics at Kobe University, but unlike you, they were mostly serious and excellent students. Most of them went on to work at banks or trading companies. I tried a lot of different things in my seminar classes to impart skills in them that they would find useful after they started working. There was one year when I had five or six students who were also in the American football club. They didn't study that much, but they had gumption, and they all found jobs at good companies. Thinking back on it now, I wish I had motivated my students more to do what they enjoyed. I wish I could have fostered more entrepreneurs.

Hiroshi: There are some famous entrepreneurs among Kobe University graduates.

Ryoichi: Sazo Idemitsu of Idemitsu Oil & Gas Co., Ltd., was in the first class to graduate from Kobe Higher Commercial School [which later became Kobe University of Commerce, Kobe University of Economics, and then Kobe University]. He was an entrepreneur through and through. One of the founding members of Suzuki Shoten, which founded Kobe Steel, Ltd., graduated from Kobe Higher Commercial School as well, and I heard that he built the business by hiring some Kobe University graduates.

Hiroshi: A lot of entrepreneurs came out of Kobe after World War II.

Ryoichi: The situation right after the war was amazing.
It started with the export of cotton. There was a time
when most of the managers of the trading companies
located in Osaka—like Marubeni, Nichimen, ITOCHU
Corporation, Kanematsu, and Ataka Sangyo—came from
Kobe University. The start of this was the import of
sheep's wool from Australia by Kanematsu. In line with
the wishes of the company's founder, Fusajiro Kanematsu,
after his passing, the company built Kanematsu Memorial
Hall at Kobe University and Kanematsu Auditorium at
Hitotsubashi University.

The Founding of Rakuten

Hiroshi: I also have entrepreneur's blood in my veins. I'm
often compared to Masayoshi Son, the leader of SoftBank,
and because he has revealed that his family is South
Korean–Japanese, some people on the Internet have
started the rumor that I'm South Korean–Japanese, too.
That would make you South Korean. [laughs]

Ryoichi: People are writing that? You are the product of
mixing between a lot of different families, including
the Hondas. We are the descendants of one of Ieyasu
Tokugawa's "four heavenly kings," Tadakatsu Honda, you
know. He was a warrior and a businessman, too, around
what is now Kobe.

Hiroshi: He possessed entrepreneurial spirit.

Ryoichi: Our family also mixed with the Urashimas.
Setsuko's father, Hideo Urashima, was a prodigy who
graduated from Kobe Higher Commercial School and
Hitotsubashi University before working in trading at
Mitsubishi Corporation. He was also the classmate
of Ichiro Nakayama while he was at Hitotsubashi,

and Mr. Nakayama later became president of Hitotsubashi University.

Hiroshi: Dr. Nakayama was the mentor of Dr. Hanawa, who was in charge of teaching the seminar class I took at Hitotsubashi University.

Ryoichi: Yes, there is a connection there. The Mikitani family also worked as wholesale rice dealers in Kobe. We have been involved in a wide range of businesses. Kobe, like Yokohama, has been a center of foreign trade since the Meiji era. And as such, there are many Europeans, Americans, visiting Chinese merchants, and Taiwanese there. That is why I had no reservations about going abroad whatsoever. I think it is because I was raised in Kobe. If I had been raised in Tokyo or Nagoya, I may have hesitated.

Hiroshi: In that sense, I think we need to return to the mind-set they had during the age of discovery. Japan must endeavor to become explorers once again.

Ryoichi: I can still remember when you made the decision to start a company. You told me that you wanted to talk to me about something. It was just before you quit your job at the Industrial Bank of Japan, and you came to stay with us in Kobe. We were living farther apart then, with you in Tokyo and us still in Kobe, so we couldn't meet each other very often, and so I wasn't sure what you would want to talk to me about. When you told me that you were going to quit your job, I remember advising you to reconsider. I asked you to rethink what you were doing at the Industrial Bank of Japan and suggested that you work to revitalize the bank from the inside. I knew a lot of people in research divisions at major banks, including the head of the research division at the Industrial Bank of Japan.

Hiroshi: And I answered that I thought it would take decades for the bank to be revitalized.

Ryoichi: I was concerned because the bank had been so good to you—letting you study abroad at Harvard Business School and then letting you study mergers and assets as well at a securities firm on Wall Street in New York after that.

Hiroshi: That was right at the time that the structure of the banking industry was changing. People were trying to create a business model that could make a profit out of buying and selling bonds in addition to charging interest on loans. I explained to you that I thought I had paid back my debts because I had made so much money for them.

Ryoichi: You said that, regardless, you were going to quit your job and start a new business. That was when you hadn't narrowed your idea down to exactly what you wanted to do, though.

Hiroshi: I had a lot of ideas. I even thought that I might be able to make a restaurant business that could create the kind of cafeterias they had on the Harvard campus.

Ryoichi: I had never even considered starting a business, so there wasn't much I could do to give you advice. I do remember though that sometime after that, I was the one who told you that you should use the name Rakuten from among the list of candidates, because you could remember it after just seeing it once.

Hiroshi: What did you think about the Internet shopping business model back then?

Ryoichi: Personally, I didn't actively take to the Internet or e-mail. So while I understood the logic of it, I thought it was going to be really difficult to order and buy something using e-mail. I had some savings then, and I told you that you could borrow from us if you needed extra funding, but you never did.

Hiroshi: Instead, I asked if you could introduce me to anyone who would want to open a store on Rakuten, and you introduced one of your students. Of the 13 merchants that opened shops on Rakuten in 1997, one of them was one of your students.

Ryoichi: I couldn't do anything else to help you. I mean, I thought it was the least I could do. One of my seminar class students went on to take on his family's business in Osaka, which was a toy wholesaler, so I asked him for a favor. His company went bankrupt due to competition with a foreign firm that entered the market here sometime after that, so he's an employee at a toy company now.

Hiroshi: What did you think about the challenge I was confronting?

Ryoichi: I admired what you were doing, albeit with a mentality of positivity, independence, and the hope that it would work out. You seemed to have really thought out what you did and didn't want to do. You were convinced of what you were doing. You had also really observed the realities of business. Furthermore, I never heard you say a mean word about anyone. I think one of your strengths is your ability to keep on trying and keep your chin up even if you fail once or twice. We took it kind of easy when we raised you, since you were the youngest. [laughs] That approach seems to have been a success.

The Evaluation System for Teachers

Hiroshi: I think we need a better evaluation system for teachers if we are going to create frameworks that don't just push knowledge but instead create the desire to study within the students themselves. With this idea in mind, we are now considering introducing a 360-degree evaluation system for personnel evaluations at Rakuten. With such systems, people in superior positions do not just evaluate their subordinates—subordinates also evaluate their superiors. I've heard the opinion that this risks the possibility that management will start to act in populist ways just to please their subordinates. But I think it's the correct choice to put a new evaluation system into place in terms of looking at things from a macro perspective.

Another idea is the peer-to-peer evaluation system—in other words, under this system teachers would evaluate their colleagues. It would be great to just ask people whether they thought the way that their colleagues taught was good or bad. We need a fundamental change in the evaluation system for teachers.

Ryoichi: It's pretty hard to evaluate teachers at universities. Everyone has a different specialty, so it is impossible for their managers to evaluate a subordinate's research. And for that reason, I think it is extremely important to have the kind of peer-to-peer evaluation system that you are talking about. There are also cases in which teachers are teaching very advanced theories, but the students don't actually understand it. So we need to evaluate teaching styles as well.

Hiroshi: Teachers at universities must do this with one another.

Ryoichi: University teachers need not teach down to the students, but they do need to come up with ways to make it so that the students understand what is being taught. I'm also thinking about my own failures here when I say that. If you see students looking around the room or spacing out during lecture, then they don't understand the material. In the United States, they pay a good amount of attention to the way lectures are given. I wish that Japanese universities would address this in a more structured way.

Hiroshi: There are also study methods that match the needs of people who are learning the material via the Internet. For example, in Denmark, students work in front of computers at their schools and receive individualized instruction for different problems, even though they are in the same mathematics class. There is also what is called *social learning*—participants undertake interactive studies and join group discussions through the Internet, and they improve their skills this way.

   The thing is, if people decide to become mere workers after they graduate, they will find themselves in positions in which they no longer feel the need to study or desire to grow. That is why we need to come up with ways for people to do more creative work. That especially will help people to become international businesspeople, but there is also a need for everyone to develop greater specializations, no matter what that specialization is.

Ryoichi: Yes, definitely. Like the *Meister* apprenticeship system they have in Germany.

Hiroshi: To that end as well, we need to bring the Japanese labor market to the world. Even if people are blue-collar workers, take them to a factory in the United States or Southeast Asia, and they have the added value of being able to work as instructors and teach technical skills.

The Need for Strategy in the Japanese Education System

Hiroshi: Although we talk about education as a single entity, there are actually many types of education, including human education, intellectual education, and education to enhance technical skills. Look around the world—for instance, look at India. The children there have been placed in a very competitive situation, with places that help them build their skills little by little and places that give education like one would find in Scandinavian countries, where they use advanced initiatives to enhance creativity. There are many patterns of education.

I am constantly thinking about education in Japan. It is not strategic. There are no goals set for the development of education here. The government's curriculum guidelines are set once every 10 years, and education proceeds in a uniform manner based on that teaching policy. Creativity is not fostered in places of education. I fear that we have an environment in our schools that does not even accept creativity. I think flexibility has always been a requirement for education. I think it would be good to have many types of schools—those that make progress on teaching using the principles of competition and those that implement creative educational initiatives.

The first point I want to make is that we should prioritize freedom of choice over a uniform education. The second point is that we need to invest in education. We need to reconceptualize education. It should not be thought of as an expense but an investment. It is particularly crucial that we create a robust educational system with a much larger number of teachers.

We need to evolve, moving away from uniform, unidirectional, and ineffective education toward the creation of an interactive, customizable education system using the Internet. We must make investments to that end. At the same time, we should change the current framework of education, including the issue of the government's curriculum guidelines and the issue of lifelong employment and the Japan Teachers' Union. Because there is a need to move education toward a more progressive direction. I believe that it is crucial for us to create an educational program that features English and IT in addition to reading, writing, and arithmetic.

Ryoichi: I am in absolute agreement with you. Investments are something that should be made in people, not things, because investments in people will produce amazing results. I find it very odd that Japanese people do not invest in education, but think of it as an expense. Why do people in Japan think that way?

Hiroshi: The opinion that education is an expense reflects an education that is given to everyone in a uniform way. The Japanese system provides all students with an education of a set standard. There are aspects of that system that surpass the systems used in other countries, but we are now in an era of international competition and an era of creativity, and within that, our young people are now facing a moratorium situation. When your own country has a low position in the world, everyone works together to outcompete other countries. But when you are in a high position already, I think there is a sense of confusion as to why we would need to work hard or compete with each other.

Ryoichi: I am most worried about the complacency among the youth.

Hiroshi: Dr. William S. Clark of Sapporo Agricultural College [currently Hokkaido University] once remarked, "Boys, be ambitious," but I think the influence of those words has been lost. With the current system, one in which people act according to instructions, students are commanded to do what they are told. And this complacent education system also tells people that they need not compete with each other.

Ryoichi: I agree.

Hiroshi: I feel like even at the elite NADA Senior High School of Hyogo Prefecture, there is a strong, rough atmosphere that you just don't see at Azabu or Kaisei in Tokyo. The students are ambitious, and they have spirit. Maybe it has something to do with the school being founded by a sake brewery? [laughs]

Ryoichi: I've always thought of the school as a gathering of a lot of excellent students. Has it changed from the way it used to be in the past?

Hiroshi: NADA Senior High School sends a lot of students to universities overseas. I've heard that a lot of the students there aim to get into Harvard, and the principal is giving them recommendations.

Ryoichi: The principal is pushing the students overseas.

Hiroshi: In terms of English education, if we just adopted TOEFL as a part of examinations to enter universities, the world would change tremendously. It's pretty hard to do difficult things, so I am always looking for things we can change that would affect a lot of other things through something like a domino effect. I think the adoption of TOEFL for university entrance examinations is one of these kinds of ideas.

Ryoichi: If we used TOEFL for university entrance exams, it would certainly lower the hurdle faced by Japanese high school students trying to enter universities overseas.

Hiroshi: Exactly. That's the important point. Like I said earlier [Chapter 4], bureaucrats have called for the adoption of "TOEFL, etc.," but they kept that word "etc." I am dead set against that word, but then their explanation is that they are not thinking of EIKEN when they say "etc.," but were trying to make considerations for qualifications tests used by Cambridge or Oxford. They said that the British embassy complained about the idea, but I think it's just an excuse. [laughs] If we are going to use an English test for university entrance exams, then it must be TOEFL. I think the inclusion of TOEFL in our entrance exams could change the world.

Ryoichi: I am basically in agreement with you about using TOEFL for entrance exams. I think a lot of hard labor is now going toward creating exam questions unique to each university, and, furthermore, some of the questions that make it into these tests are weird. So I'm in agreement about TOEFL, but how do you propose to use it?

Hiroshi: Some universities have already announced that they are adopting TOEFL as a part of their entrance exams.

Ryoichi: The English teachers making the questions for entrance exams should at least be happy.

Hiroshi: Those teachers are now working very hard to study TOEFL. After all, what will they do if someone asks them what their TOEFL score is? [laughs]

Ryoichi: Where is TOEFL created in the United States?

Hiroshi: It's a program being developed by Educational Testing Services (ETS), a nonprofit organization located in New Jersey. When they were told that we wanted to use the test for university entrance exams, they said that they would charge 15,000 yen per person. The Ministry of Education, Culture, Sports, Science and Technology replied that the cost was too high, and now at Rakuten we are in negotiation with ETS, and we're trying to lower the price to 3,000 yen with the promise that tens of thousands of students will take it. ETS has said that they aren't sure if they can do it for 3,000 yen, but they have promised to lower the price for us.

I believe that if students can get into Harvard or Stanford thanks to their TOEFL scores, they can think about new dreams. Young people today don't have the dream of being active on the international stage, but that would change if they knew people were becoming active internationally. It's just like it was with the U.S. Major League Baseball (MLB). When Hideo Nomo went to go play for the Los Angeles Dodgers, people said that a Japanese player could never be successful in the MLB. But after he started playing, that mind-set changed. People realized that Japanese players could be successful.

Ryoichi: After a few people become successful overseas, it won't be long before the whole flow of students from one school to the other changes.

Hiroshi: Right now the school with the highest number of students succeeding at the University of Tokyo entrance exam is Kaisei Senior High School. When we reach a point where the top 10 students there are deciding to go to Harvard instead of the University of Tokyo, then the mind-set of students as a whole will make a 180-degree turn. And if the best Japanese students choose to forgo Japanese universities, then that will also put a very good kind of pressure on universities in Japan.

Ryoichi: The University of Tokyo was considered allowing students to start school in the autumn, which would make it easier for students coming from overseas to go there, but I've heard that they gave up on the idea. This is unfortunate; I think if the University of Tokyo had started doing that, then the idea would have spread to other universities as well. According to the newspaper reports, they gave up on the idea because letting people enter in September would disadvantage them when it came time for exams to become a public employee or lawyer.

Hiroshi: I think the real reason is the change in presidents at the University of Tokyo. The former president, Hiroshi Komiyama, came up with the idea to allow students to start in the autumn. I understand it as being that sort of thing. [laughs] I can also understand the logic that if no other universities make that change, then the University of Tokyo can't possibly be the only one doing it. It's just like how they won't change from using inches and yards to the metric system in the United States. In the end, it's difficult for only one school to change the time when it lets students in. I think there's a need to resolve to make that kind of change on a national level.

Ryoichi: It's definitely something to be discussed at a national level. I suppose it would be difficult for just one school to do that.

Hiroshi: In April 2013, Rakuten hired 306 new graduates. Of those, 18 graduated from the University of Tokyo. That is roughly the same number as the number of University of Tokyo graduates who chose to enter the Industrial Bank of Japan in the same year I was hired. We can't know why these people chose to work at Rakuten unless we ask them individually. But because we set English as our common working language, the number of people coming from the University of Tokyo is increasing. I believe that we may be attracting students who want to start their own business eventually in the future.

Ryoichi: I think it is excellent to have a lot of young employees come in with entrepreneurial and international mind-sets.

Summary

- Dramatically reform the one-sided didactic structure of education and develop a creative and diverse educational system.
- Teach English from elementary school onward.
- Use the Internet to create interactive education.
- Create a peer-to-peer evaluation system for teachers.
- Make TOEFL a part of university entrance examinations.

7 | The Power to Build Brand Japan

Brand Power

Hiroshi: I want to talk about brand power. When I say brand power, I am thinking of premium earning power. Even among similar products, there are differences in value among products with a brand and those without one. Made in Japan, for example, is a brand, and one that I think still has value, although not as much as it used to have. One reason for that is the widespread proliferation of IT networks. Global gaps in information and design are closing.

Beyond that, and separate from product brands, there is the brand value of Japan. This can be measured by how many tourists visit each year, how many global companies base their headquarters here, and how attractive Japan is as a country. If many tourists visit and many companies build their headquarters in Japan, then the image people have of Japanese products will rise as a matter of course, and people will also start to feel greater attraction to Japanese fashion. I feel like we often think of the brand value of countries and brand value of products as different concepts, but in this way, I think the two values are synchronized.

Ryoichi: I agree.

Hiroshi: How can we tie together the brand of a country with product brands? At New Economy Summit 2013 held by Japan Association of New Economy, many of the foreign participants told us about their love of Japan. But if we look at the big picture, such favorable feelings are not being reflected in the value of Japanese products. I think this is in part due to bad marketing. The work to spread our brand value over a wide area has not been very good. A lot has been done at the national level, like the "Cool Japan" initiative. But I have the strong impression that with the initiatives so far, it has been a case of too many cooks spoiling the broth; they have been trying to include everything, and there has not been a robust strategy. Even though there has been wide financing for this initiative—to the tune of hundreds of millions or billions of yen—our initiatives haven't been effective. It may be that the Japanese strategy has been "spiced" incorrectly.

Ryoichi: Perhaps it just lacks spice completely.

Hiroshi: For example, we can look at 2011 data from the United Nations World Tourism Organization and see the revenue resulting from tourists visiting the countries in the Asia-Pacific region. China's revenue was the highest, with approximately U.S. $48.5 billion. The next highest earner was Australia, followed by Hong Kong. Japan was ranked 10th on that list, taking in approximately U.S. $11 billion. That is just one-fifth of the money taken in by

China, and a figure lower than [those of] South Korea and Taiwan. Obviously, we need to enhance the attractiveness of our tourism resources and actively implement marketing activities.

Ryoichi: The data on foreign visitors to Japan is shocking.

Hiroshi: The biggest problem there is visas. Unless we greatly relax visa restrictions and allow more foreign tourists to enter Japan without a visa, I don't think we can ever see a big increase in the number of people who come here. But if we do that, people start to ask about the issue of illegal labor. To a certain extent, I think that kind of "cost" can't be helped.

Ryoichi: We need to bring greater compassion to the way we tackle this issue.

Hiroshi: The reasons that revenue from tourism is low are simple. We have built barriers to tourism, and we don't give out visas. Also, we can try and talk to foreign nationals about the appeal of the traditional culture of Japan, but if people don't understand the terms we are using, our efforts are in vain. We need to promote the best points of Japan in ways that are easier for people to understand.

I think sumo is the best example of what I am talking about here. Currently, a lot of the wrestlers in the top three sumo ranks, the *yokozunas* and so forth, are Mongolian. When the Ministry of Foreign Affairs conducted an *Image of Japan Study in Mongolia* in 2004, asking people about the "country with which Mongolia should be friendly," Japan took the top spot with 37 percent of the responses, followed by the United States in second place at 35 percent, Russia at 28 percent, and South Korea at 14 percent. In other words, Japan was ranked far higher than China or South Korea, even higher than the United States. And I think the reason behind the

popularity of Japan in Mongolia is the wide reporting
that the Official Development Assistance of the Japanese
government gets within the country and the intense
exchanges that take place between these countries in
relation to sumo. When they asked "Which famous
people in Japan do you like?" four of the top five
responses were sumo wrestlers.

Ryoichi: That's amazing!

Hiroshi: Mongolians have come to know about Japan
through sumo, and they have developed the image that
Japan is a good country. That is why I've proposed that we
eliminate the quota system for foreign athletes in sports
like Japanese professional baseball and football.

Ryoichi: The restriction on the number of foreign players
still exists?

Hiroshi: It still exists even in Japanese professional football
and other sports. I could understand it if we were talking
about high school baseball, but I can't understand why we
need to have a restriction system for foreign athletes in
professional sports. I just don't get it.

Ryoichi: We aren't talking about amateurs, after all.

Hiroshi: I think if we had Chinese and South Korean
athletes come to Japan and excel at sports here, then their
efforts would be broadcast widely on television, satellite
television, and the Internet, and people would naturally
start to feel a greater affinity with Japan. It's not like the
World Cup or the Olympics or other such competitions,
because at those events there is the strong feeling that we
are participating in an international competition, so they
aren't very good for increasing feelings of friendship
among nations.

Ryoichi: Because people think of the events as being
competitions pitting their country against other countries.
From that perspective, I think the Wimbledon

tournament held each year in the suburbs of London as one of the Grand Slam tennis tournaments is an excellent event.

Hiroshi: Andy Murray from the United Kingdom won Wimbledon for the first time in the summer of 2013 by beating out Novak Djokovic from Serbia. It was in fact the first time in 77 years that a player from the United Kingdom had won. That tournament draws the top players and lovers of tennis from around the world. Everyone goes to watch the tournament each time it is held. The UK royal family even attends and has the top players, dressed as they are in white from head to toe, bow and curtsy before them. [laughs] Even if their own athletes don't win, I think the tournament is doing plenty to increase the UK brand.

Decisions about marketing strategy are made on the basis of intuition, so I think there is a need to have people with a good sense for that kind of thing to think strategically about how to enhance the brand and fashion of Japan. On the contrary, the current approach by the Japanese government is to have the Ministry of Economy, Trade and Industry (METI) take the lead in creating a fund and then gather a group that they are accustomed to working with, including the major advertising firms of Japan, to carry out various initiatives. They seem to be responding not with quality, but with quantitative expansion. I think it's just awful, really terrible.

Another important thing that we need to do is convince global corporations to build headquarters in Japan. Look at the United Kingdom and the UK Trade & Investment, which offers incentives to convince corporations that they should place their headquarters in London. In Japan, even though we were once home to the Asia headquarters of companies like Procter & Gamble

and Nestlé, most of those companies have now moved
overseas.

Ryoichi: I suppose they are leaving Japan and moving to
Southeast Asia.

Hiroshi: I think a lot of them moved to Singapore. So
winning headquarters means beating Singapore. [laughs]
What's our argument for bringing Asian headquarters to
Japan? For a start, Singapore is unbearably hot, there isn't
much space for offices, and the living environment in
Japan is absolutely better.

The Demonstration Effect

Hiroshi: When thinking about branding, it's useful to
consider the demonstration effect. I touched on this topic
earlier [Chapter 1]. It's a concept posited by Dr. James
Duesenberry, who was a Harvard University professor.

Ryoichi: Yes. Schumpeter was the dean of the economics
department at Harvard after World War II, and he
mentored a lot of people during his time there, among
them students who went on to become remarkable
economists. Duesenberry was one of the most notable.
Duesenberry, like Schumpeter, made a significant
contribution to the analysis of Keynesian economics.

To explain Keynesian economics in rough terms, it
states that if you want to increase employment, all you
need to do is stimulate the economy through such means
as increasing investment—for example, by lowering
interest rates. Keynes also talked about the *marginal efficiency
of capital*, which is a concept that recommends that
governments improve the investment environment and
implement policies that enhance investment efficiency. It
was common in macroeconomics after World War II to

advocate for the implementation of structural policies in order to promote investment, including with regard to financial policies.

But then right after that the consumption-function controversy emerged. General consumption is determined by the aggregation of income, but there was a fierce debate about whether factors other than income influenced that and how the consumption function should be set. That debate started after the war, at around 1950. It was a major theme of macroeconomics right when I was beginning my career as an academic, back when I was still in graduate school. Duesenberry was one of the main players in the consumption-function controversy, and within his arguments he advanced the two new concepts of the demonstration effect and ratchet effect. Both were major contributions to economics.

He pushed for the idea that consumption is not determined by income alone. You can tell what kind of consumption activities a single person is going to do by looking at their income and the consumption function, but the problem is that people do not participate in economic activities on an isolated island only while living by themselves. They also undertake consumption activities with their neighbors. Duesenberry believed that people felt feedback from society.

This may not be apparent if you are looking at something like the amount that people spend on food when they eat at home, but you can easily see this if we are talking about when people buy automobiles or the latest and trendiest fashion, because we have a large data source of people who drive cars or wear clothes when they go out. People see other people wearing fashionable clothes, and they begin to think that they want to buy those clothes. Then they do. That is what Duesenberry called the "demonstration effect."

His second idea that I want to talk about was the "ratchet effect," which is similar to the demonstration effect. It describes the consumption activity by which people refuse to go to restaurants that serve bad food after they have experienced good food at a fancier place. Once people have experienced or purchased something nice, they will continue to spend the same amount of money for it if they can receive the same experience or product. That choice is the consumption activity described by the ratchet effect. These two ideas are considered Duesenberry's most famous achievements, and I think they contributed a great deal to the consumption-function controversy after World War II.

Another thing that Duesenberry is famous for is the relative income hypothesis. The income of a single person is not determined independently of other variables; it is actually affected by the relative size of other people's incomes, and it rises and falls in relation to those other income levels. This is similar to the demonstration effect. That idea was also a major contribution to American macroeconomics.

Now, this is all based on empirical research. From the 1950s to the mid-1960s, there was fierce debate about whether the theories could be organized and consolidated. But then a new debate emerged from the 1970s—this time about inflation. From the latter half of the 1960s, inflation became a real problem, and so from the beginning of the 1970s onward, people started to debate the issue. Many different ideas were put forward during this time, with there again being fierce debate about whether a certain amount of inflation wasn't actually good for capitalism, or whether the inflation rate shouldn't in fact be zero. The Chicago school of economists called for the establishment of an appropriate amount of inflation.

Hiroshi: You mean Milton Friedman.

Ryoichi: Yes. Milton Friedman was the leader of the Chicago school. And on the other side of that, the Keynesians called for inflation to be zero. James Tobin pressed this idea. This argument continued over five years as a central topic of economics around the world. In Japan, Dr. Chiaki Nishiyama at Rikkyo University was the spokesperson for Friedman.

Friedman came up with the permanent income hypothesis to counter Duesenberry's relative income hypothesis. This idea states that the basis for judgments about consumption activities is individuals' expectations about their income over the course of their whole lifetime—not just their incomes at certain times. Looked at over the course of a whole lifetime, there are times when people's income is good and times when it is bad, and people make logical decisions based on predictions about that. When income grows, people save more, and when it falls, people use their savings to make up the difference. That is what the hypothesis states. So because consumption is determined based on permanent income, it is thought that a certain portion of income will be kept. And part of what this means is, because people are rational, when they die they will inevitably leave behind a lot of assets. Milton Friedman's hypothesis posits that people won't save the large amount of money resulting from those assets, but will use them for consumption.

Hiroshi: But how do the demonstration effect and consumption-function controversy, or the battle about inflation, connect to our discussion about branding?

Ryoichi: Right, right, we were talking about branding weren't we? [laughs] What relates to branding here is the demonstration effect. The ratchet effect may be related to a certain extent as well, but the important idea here is the demonstration effect. What happens to that demonstration effect when branding comes into the picture is not something that was debated when the idea was first being discussed. It would be a good theme for a young researcher with an interest in this kind of thing, I think.

Brand Value at the National Level

Hiroshi: Given what you have been saying, if we are to accept the permanent income hypothesis of the Chicago school, then, well, to put it negatively, permanent income is kind of predetermined. So it doesn't matter if we have branding or not.

Ryoichi: Some people have made criticisms, saying things like, because we have brands, and because brands see what other brands are doing, a lot of different cases emerge in the actual economy. Whether that has an impact on consumption activities is a very interesting academic theme. It would be nice if a young economist would take it up.

Hiroshi: I believe that Japan's brand is extremely important in terms of theories of trade and comparative advantage.

Ryoichi: Yes. In economics, people think about controversies within closed systems. The next step is naturally that we must think about these ideas in terms of open systems, including how the ideas affect other countries and trade, just like you are saying. If we are talking about an open system, then I think there will also be differences in the demonstration effect and ratchet effect because consumption activities and culture differ in each country.

Hiroshi: I don't know if it has to do with the demonstration effect or not, but once South Korea started to export its media contents more, such as its dramas, that media started to get popular in the countries where they were exported to. And when that happened, people started to buy Samsung televisions and South Korean clothes, too, because they thought the South Korean actors were cool. I think in doing so, they not only increased the brand power of individual products, but also, in fact, enhanced the value of the Made in Korea brand by associating products with other things.

Ryoichi: You might call it a ripple effect.

Hiroshi: In that sense, I believe that brand value at a national level enhances the brand value of products. What do you think?

Ryoichi: National-level brand value may certainly have the sway to pull other brand values up or down. And that may be true for the Made in Japan brand as well—even for automobiles. I think Japanese products have brand value.

Hiroshi: Japanese products are definitely high quality. With cars, I think, for instance, Toyota sells more cars when its vehicles win F1 races. That is really the demonstration effect in practice, isn't it? It impacts the way that people differentiate Toyota's products. And furthermore, I believe that it's a fact that as the image people have of Japan as a nation improves, the image they have of Japanese products improves as well.

Ryoichi: That's certainly true. I do think that when there is an improvement in image across the board, it improves the image of individual products.

Hiroshi: In 2012, I made a trip to Singapore, and I was shocked to see that Samsung TVs were priced higher than

the Sony or Panasonic sets there. I thought that Samsung
was selling its home electronics at cheaper prices, but that
wasn't the case. In fact, Sony, Panasonic, and Sharp TVs
were cheaper.

Ryoichi: You don't say? What about the performance?

Hiroshi: In terms of the performance, too—the Samsung
sets were selling at a higher price.

Ryoichi: The Samsung TVs also had good performance
then?

Hiroshi: The reason for that is that Samsung has pursued
research and development with a focus on global TV
standards, so their TVs perform well in terms of the
functions that people around the world want to use, like
Smart TV features. Japanese TVs, on the other hand, have
good resolution, but they can't compete with the features
available on TVs that meet global standards. This is
another Galapagos situation—people can watch
high-resolution footage only in Japan. There is not really
any connection being made to global standards.

Ryoichi: In other words, in terms of technology, we've
already reached a point where national borders don't
matter.

Hiroshi: In particular, with heavy and chemical industry
products, it isn't just that the technology has gone global,
it's that companies overseas possess a higher level of
technology than we have in Japan.

Ryoichi: Well, that's a problem. But to what extent do you
think Japanese people realize that?

Hiroshi: No, I mean, I don't really think that people do
realize it.

Ryoichi: In that case, then it's like I said earlier
[Chapter 5]—it's extremely important that we make clear
to what extent the management at Sharp, for example,

realize the reality of their situation, and if they do realize it, how they are responding to that. And if they aren't responding, why not? We live in an era in which speed wins the day. If you are too late with something, it can be difficult to recover.

Hiroshi: Recovery is already impossible.

Ryoichi: I don't know if it's impossible or not, but I think it's difficult. The point I'm trying to emphasize is whether or not the management of major corporations realize the situation that they are in. If they do, and they can't mount a response to it, then I think we need to investigate where the problem here really lies.

Hiroshi: Because the brand value of Japanese products is in part based on the brand of Japan as a nation, I think we need to improve the image that people have of Japan. And I don't just mean talking about Japan's brand by itself—I also think that we need to tell the world loud and clear that Japan is not just a safe country, it's also a place where the food is delicious and the fashion is cool. The government has done a lot of different things for this, but I feel like they are approaching this from the perspective that all they need to do is spend money, while marketing is something that should really be done strategically.

Ryoichi: That's no good.

Hiroshi: So, for example, at the U.S. embassy in Japan, the ambassador will hold banquets when CEOs of American IT companies visit, and will invite important people from the worlds of politics, finance, and the bureaucracy in order to deepen exchange. They do this at the French and Italian embassies, too. I have often been invited to those banquets. But when I go abroad? I have rarely been invited to a banquet hosted by a local Japanese ambassador. Are there any Japanese embassies doing that kind of thing overseas?

Ryoichi: There is a business community who have a lot of contact with the bureaucrats of the Ministry of Foreign Affairs. Maybe they are only inviting those people?

Hiroshi: Yes, it may only be that I'm just not invited to take part in those kinds of missions. In Japan, the Ministry of Foreign Affairs, the METI, and the Ministry of Finance are all part of a vertical structure and working in different directions. Food is being handled by the Ministry of Agriculture, Forestry and Fisheries; culture is being handled by the Agency for Cultural Affairs at the Ministry of Education, Culture, Sports, Science and Technology; tourism is handled by the Ministry of Land, Infrastructure, Transport and Tourism; and science and technology marketing is handled by the METI. No single person is looking at the entirety of the situation.

Ryoichi: That's not a problem of the brand image of Japan; it's a problem that has seeped into every policy.

Hiroshi: That is why I believe that we must think of comprehensive promotions that stretch beyond the role and purpose of each ministry if we are going to enhance our national brand image. One part of this is communications toward other countries. Another important part of it is efforts to draw foreign nationals to Japan and to invite foreign companies to base their headquarters in Japan. What I'm about to say differs a little from the ratchet effect concept that you talked about, but I think if we get people to come to Japan and experience for themselves the deliciousness of Japanese food and excellence of Japanese cars, they will learn to love Japanese products and they will start to buy them. I don't believe that anyone would drive a Hyundai after they've had the experience of driving a Toyota.

Ryoichi: I agree.

Hiroshi: Conversely, the value of our consumer electronics—our TVs and so forth—is disappearing. One might say that we are seeing a diminishing ratchet effect there.

Ryoichi: I believe that the product that left the biggest impression on people of all the Japanese goods that debuted after World War II was the Sony Walkman. There was nothing else like it when it first came out. Thinking of it now, they made radios more compact.

Hiroshi: It was a radio and cassette tape player.

Ryoichi: Yes, exactly. And you could record audio with it.

Hiroshi: When the Sony Walkman came out it conquered the world. And doing so, Sony's brand improved. I think entrepreneurs create brand power like that. In Sony's case, it was Akio Morita and Norio Ohga. In Apple's case, it was Steve Jobs. In Samsung's case, it was the vice chairman of Samsung electronics Jae-Yong Lee. He's part of the third generation of the family that founded the company, and he's an excellent businessperson.

The single improvement in Samsung's brand image has made it rapidly more competitive on the world stage. There is no doubt in my mind that people who like Samsung products buy other South Korean goods. It is an extremely natural thing to do.

Foreign Nationals Working in Japan

Hiroshi: It is estimated that about 8.3 million foreign nationals visit Japan each year. This is a far lower figure than the number of people who visit Singapore, China, and South Korea. Because of that, I think it is extremely important that we get even more people to visit Japan and understand the good points of our country.

Another issue here is having foreign nationals work in Japan. When foreign nationals work in Japan, it increases the feelings of affection that people overseas feel toward us. I think the best way to make use of this effect is through sports. It's also great to have Japanese players actively playing sports overseas—as is being done by Ichiro in the U.S. MLB and Shinji Kagawa at Manchester United in the United Kingdom, but I think it's best to have foreign players come to Japan, to deepen our person-to-person exchanges, and raise interest in Japan that way.

That is why I want to get rid of the foreign player restrictions in professional sports like soccer and baseball in Japan, as I stated earlier. I don't think there is anything wrong with foreigners.

Ryoichi: But what if every athlete ended up being from overseas?

Hiroshi: Even that would be fine. But that will never happen. [laughs] Rakuten has been growing rapidly in Taiwan, and our brand is well known among Taiwanese people. One reason for that is two Taiwanese players, Ying-chieh Lin and En-yu Lin, are playing for the Tohoku Rakuten Golden Eagles, and their games are broadcast every day in Taiwan. For J. League soccer [Japanese professional football], too, at the very least we should get rid of the restriction for players from Asia. If athletes from around Asia played in Japan, J. League games would start to be broadcast on the television stations of each country.

If we can get more players like Andruw Jones, who came from the New York Yankees to play for the Tohoku Rakuten Golden Eagles—if we can get more people like that to come and play in Japan, it will be interesting for people from a content perspective, it will increase revenue from television broadcasts, and it will increase the interest that people overseas feel toward Japan. It kills three birds with one stone.

Ryoichi: I wonder if Americans would watch professional baseball games in Japan if American players were more active here.

Hiroshi: They absolutely would. And the level of pro baseball in Japan would improve.

Ryoichi: For some reason or another, we don't see the same thing happening with pro baseball that we have seen with sumo. Sumo wouldn't be any fun without the Mongolians.

Hiroshi: It would be a dull sport. It would be such a killjoy to have it be a contest of only Japanese people. Because Mongolians are better in terms of speed and skill, and so you start to get people who train even harder, with all of their might, trying to figure out how to beat the Mongolians. It raises the level of play among Japanese wrestlers.

This isn't just about sports, though. I think the issue of how we can get foreign nationals to become endeared with Japan is extremely important. We cannot just have the foreign engineers of Rakuten or people like Carlos Ghosn at Nissan—we need more foreigners who love Japan.

Ryoichi: How did Carlos Ghosn learn to love Japan, I wonder?

Hiroshi: He was originally an immigrant. He's a business-person with a strong fighting instinct.

Ryoichi: He was originally from Brazil. Internationalism is in his blood, I suppose.

Hiroshi: Taking my argument to its extreme, I think if we had a lot of South Korean and Chinese sports stars playing professional baseball and football in Japan, we would have

never seen the development of problems with the Sentaku
Islands or Takeshima.

Ryoichi: That may be true.

Hiroshi: In particular, we need to overwhelmingly
differentiate our brand value from other Asian brands.
Because China and South Korea are so important.
This isn't a joke—I absolutely believe that we must
eliminate the restriction for at least foreign sports
professionals from Asia.

Making Japan Attractive to Foreign Nationals

Hiroshi: In any case, we have far too many ridiculous
regulations. I'm thinking here of things like regulations on
casinos and the Act on Control and Improvement of
Amusement Business, etc. that too harshly restrict the
entertainment options enjoyed by young people. Places
like Kyoto, Kamakura, and Nikko have interesting tourist
spots, but if there is nothing fun to do in these places,
people won't go.

Ryoichi: When you stay in Tokyo, you end up going to
Kamakura and Nikko. But the only people who go to
these places multiple times are those who really love
Japan. Most foreign nationals only go once.

Hiroshi: There are a lot of needs in the market, including
the need for casinos. I don't think we should have so
many regulations. Even Singapore, stern as it is, has started
to have casinos, and this has changed their national image
a lot. Even the third prime minister of the Republic of
Singapore, Lee Hsien Loong, himself the eldest son of the
first prime minister Lee Kuan Yew, has said something to
the effect that if there were no casinos in Singapore the
country's image would have worsened.

Ryoichi: His father, Lee Kuan Yew, was a fastidious and extremely regimented man. Did something change with his son's generation?

Hiroshi: It was apparently a big shock for the people of Singapore, too.

Ryoichi: I imagine it would be.

Hiroshi: But by building just two casinos, they increased the number of tourists they receive annually by over two million people.

Ryoichi: Really? That's a real success story.

Hiroshi: When people from Singapore enter the casino, they are required to pay a special tax just to get in. I think it's about 7,000 yen.

Ryoichi: At that rate, most people wouldn't be able to go.

Hiroshi: The general populace doesn't go in. They play mah-jongg at local parlors. [laughs]

Ryoichi: I suppose more people would go to the casinos if they made it cheaper to enter.

Hiroshi: The point is that the casinos were built to attract people from overseas. If we did the same thing here, we could draw a lot of foreign tourists to Japan.

Ryoichi: I think it would also go pretty well if we made it possible to do medical tourism here.

Hiroshi: That is just like the sale of pharmaceuticals over the Internet—in the end, it's all a matter of where we draw the line for our regulations. The Ministry of Health, Labour and Welfare doesn't want to approve medical tourism, because they think it will lead to an approval of mixed medical care services.

Ryoichi: I have two personal experiences that relate to medical tourism. There is a manmade island due south of JR Sannomiya Station in Hyogo Prefecture within the Kobe port called Port Island. On this island, the city has gathered a cluster of advanced medical facilities, such as

Kobe City Medical Center General Hospital, as part of the KOBE Biomedical Innovation Cluster project. The RIKEN Advanced Institute for Computational Science, home of the fastest supercomputer in the world, the K computer, is located there. They don't do much advertising, but people who go there can receive advanced medical treatment, and they are receiving a decent amount of foreign patients from around Asia. I also noticed many foreign patients when I once visited the tourist center in Ichikawa City, Chiba Prefecture.

Hiroshi: If you're in a position of power around Asia and a Japanese doctor saves your life, you're going to learn to love Japan.

Ryoichi: That is why we should make better use of the advanced medical care available in Japan. I think we need to offer people more options beyond just immigration. People should be able to come to Japan for long-term or short-term stays as well. Put simply, because there is an international division of labor, Japan should absolutely be making use of its advanced medical care, something which is one of our major strengths, to support the economy. What's important here is how to make that possible, and where we might find breakthrough areas.

Hiroshi: Currently mixed medical care services aren't legal, so we can't do anything like build a hospital for just foreign nationals. We can only make it so that general hospitals accept foreign patients.

Ryoichi: In the end, we need to have more deregulation.

Hiroshi: A lot of foreign nationals would come to Japan if we had medical tourism here. It would become a major business. And it would improve the image of Japan. It is something we absolutely must do.

Ryoichi: I have personally received medical care at a number of different hospitals, and I can say for a fact that

Japanese medical care is excellent. What do you think of the doctors' groups here?

Hiroshi: I think there may be a lot of people in the Japan Medical Association and in the government who have a narrow outlook on things.

Ryoichi: The value of a doctor can be judged by the number of people they cure. I think they must be happy when their patients get better and think of that with a sense of pride. So I think what we are talking about is a movement that should start within the Japan Medical Association, because I have to believe that many doctors have good hearts. This is about a just cause—it is good for people and good for the people of the world, so I would hope that people would pursue this without hesitation.

Hiroshi: But consider the fact that in Japan there are still some cases of medical insurance and medical treatments being paid entirely by patients. The universal health care system is in place to address the health problems of Japanese people. We don't have the kind of system in place that we would need to allow a foreign national to come to Japan, pay money, and be cured. The issue here is that we aren't making progress on removing restrictions on mixed medical care services.

Ryoichi: We need to establish examples of success and find places where we can make real breakthroughs. Public opinion can help us along in this; progress may be easier to achieve for medical care than other topics. I have the feeling that medical tourism would be successful.

Japan and the Trans–Pacific Partnership

Hiroshi: To create an open Japan, we must not overlook the liberalization of trade and things like the Trans-Pacific

Partnership (TPP), free trade agreements (FTAs), and economic partnership agreements (EPAs). There is truly a global trend going on around the signing of FTAs. South Korea has signed FTAs with the United States and the European Union, and it's expected to continue to actively focus on signing more FTAs. Put another way, if we don't sign the TPP and FTAs, we just won't be able to participate in global competition. It isn't a matter of whether FTAs are good or bad, the issue is that we have no choice but to participate in them.

Ryoichi: Japan still hasn't joined the TPP, right?

Hiroshi: It hasn't.[1] As of July 2013, we have just managed to reach the level of participating in TPP negotiations.

Ryoichi: What's the situation with FTAs and EPAs?

Hiroshi: In terms of FTAs and EPAs, Japan has signed agreements with 13 countries and regions, including Singapore, Thailand, India, Mexico, and Switzerland. We are also in negotiation for a Japan–China–South Korea EPA and for agreements with the European Union and Canada, although we haven't even entered negotiations yet with the United States. So it is important that we participate in the TPP and, at the same time, it is also extremely important that we make progress on other FTA negotiations.

The theory of comparative advantage is the logical backbone to this point. Because each country specializes in what it excels at, the promotion of trade can make one plus one equal three. One country really shouldn't be able to excel over every other country in every single field. If that happened, bilateral diplomatic relations would be quite nasty and would stagnate. That shouldn't happen. Instead, Japan should let partner countries handle certain industries and, at the same time, aggressively export goods

---

[1] As of March 2014, Japan has not yet joined the TPP.

and services from the industries that we excel at. In doing so, we can make one plus one equal three. This is another policy that can kill three birds with one stone.

Looking at the arguments in Japan made by people who are against the TPP, it seems like most are stating their opposition by saying that their own industry will collapse if we join the partnership. In terms of the country as a whole, it may be true that certain industries will collapse, but that's fine. Other industries will flourish.

Ryoichi: That's the logic behind the theory of comparative advantage, yes. It's just like you said.

Hiroshi: We can't be trying to win at everything. I think we should be saying, "Well, this isn't profitable, but this is." What's important here is that there will be a large-scale shift in our industrial structure through participation in the TPP.

Ryoichi: So, I think it is crucial that we come to some form of agreement on these issues. It's hard to know what is going to happen in the future when you are at a crossroad. I think it is vital that we have a kind of social agreement or agreement among businesspeople saying that, for example, "We're at a crossroad, and this road is dangerous. Let's move forward on that other road."

Hiroshi: Japan is putting up a fight in industries like Internet services, video games, and anime. The way I see it, we are competitive in the industries that the bureaucracy isn't tampering with. That's why I think we will see a rise in competitiveness by deregulations.

Ryoichi: The same is true for medical care. It's the same situation.

Hiroshi: It's true for even the agricultural industry. We are exporting a tremendous amount of seafood to Hong Kong through Rakuten Ichiba. China wants to buy Japanese agricultural products.

Ryoichi: They are safe and delicious. In that sense, agriculture as well might be called a growth industry, I suppose.

Hiroshi: And for that reason, I think there is the potential for agriculture to become a giant industry if we recognize agricultural corporations and make it possible for them to purchase farmland as they like.

Ryoichi: I completely agree. I used to think of the agriculture industry as just providing us with a stable supply of rice, which is our staple food in Japan, but in fact, when we talk about agriculture, we are talking about an extremely diverse field. There is diversity in terms of the different species of livestock, diversity in product quality, and even the same types of rice can taste completely different and have different nutritional properties. And in that sense, I believe that Japanese agriculture has a future.

Safety, quality control, and deliciousness are all points that are still being worked through for the products of Southeast Asia and China. So, in a way, Japan is an advanced agricultural economy. We should lower costs as much as possible, eliminate waste in cultivation, and enhance productivity. All of this is extremely important. The Ministry of Agriculture, Forestry and Fisheries is overprotective, and I think there is a tendency for industry to be overreliant on it. I have the impression that alongside the Ministry of Finance, the Ministry of Agriculture, Forestry and Fisheries is one of our most protective organizations, and one having a very close relationship with industry.

Hiroshi: I think if people take their work seriously, Japanese agriculture is fairly competitive. Because even Chinese people don't want to eat agricultural products made in China. If the price isn't too high, people want to eat agricultural products from Japan.

Ryoichi: Definitely. We might also be able to see our agricultural products using the Japan brand.

Hiroshi: Why do you think the agricultural industry here is stagnating?

Ryoichi: Isn't it because of the Japan Agricultural Cooperatives (JA)? They are stifling innovation. And they are thick as thieves with core politicians.

Hiroshi: JA officials are like private-sector bureaucrats. We might call it JA socialism. We still have a structure that protects small farms and makes it impossible to consolidate land. It's a problem.

Ryoichi: We are being forced to make the transition in our economy from *Gemeinschaft* ("community") to *Gesellschaft* ("society"), but in doing that, I think the frameworks protecting our communities will become chains holding us back. I mean, there are farmers out there who are giving birth to innovations in agricultural technologies, but I think a lot of farmers think it's acceptable to just keep making products and selling them to JA.

Hiroshi: Another point here is that farming villages have a loud voice in politics. There is disparity in the way votes are registered for national elections. The votes cast by people living in farming communities are worth more than the votes cast by people living in cities. I think that is one reason behind the fall in Japan's competitiveness.

Ryoichi: I don't think that Japan even needs the House of Councillors. It's the remnant of our House of Peers, but we no longer have that kind of class structure in Japanese society. We have no need for that house any longer.

Hiroshi: But isn't there the risk that with only one house, there would be no check on politics and policies would become reckless? There's no doubt in my mind that the current political system has problems, including issues like the twisted Diet in which different parties control the House of Representatives and the House of Councillors. I also don't think much of having the Prime Minister change so often.

Ryoichi: It's rare across the world. What about you, Hiroshi? Ever think of becoming a politician?

Hiroshi: Never. Because I would no longer be able to spend every night drinking to my heart's content. [laughs] I'm joking about that, but the fact is that I don't think I would be able to do anything worthwhile as a politician. Even Prime Minister Abe can't exercise his authority because of the amount of people who resist his policies. I think we can see the same situation with the presidency of the United States. But then even so, we need to change politics. Even if it takes time, we must change education, we must change our national mind-set, and we must globalize the Japanese.

Ryoichi: I believe that Japanese people have the ability to do that.

Hiroshi: I do, too. Japanese people are excellent. I think people would be able to make great use of their abilities if we just eliminated regulations and liberalized. The issue is that nationalism has made our regulations too strict and turned us into an isolated state. We need to tremendously enhance Japan's competitiveness, in much the same way that we raised the competitiveness of our soccer teams to the extent that Japan could even appear in the World Cup. Nothing good comes from overprotection. If we just opened Japan more, I believe that we would triumph in many different industries. Some industries would fail, too, but I believe it is crucial that we develop in an open and fair manner.

Summary

- Strengthen the Made in Japan brand image at a national level.
- Greatly relax visa requirements and increase the number of foreign tourists to Japan.
- Increase the number of foreign firms with a head office in Japan.
- Eliminate the foreign player restrictions in professional sports and increase the number of foreign athletes in Japan.
- Facilitate an environment that is easier for foreign nationals to live in.
- Join the TPP and FTAs and promote free trade.

Conclusion

What Is the Power
to Compete?

Japan Uniquely Incorporates and Interprets Cultures

Hiroshi: Over three months, I've discussed different themes with you based on my "Japan Again" proposal. While we've been having these discussions, the Abe administration has been hard at work preparing its growth strategy, and although some of my proposals were adopted, essential issues like the restart of nuclear power stations have been set in line with the scenarios drawn up by the bureaucrats. We are now nearing the end of our debates. How have you felt about our discussions over these last three months?

Ryoichi: I fully support your proposal. The issue now is all about how we can realize it. If we could just find something that we could make a breakthrough on,

we could start from there. Our next step is crucial. How
can we switch to the new path? I think we'll need to
borrow the wisdom of many different people.

Hiroshi: We should go for the low-hanging fruit first, and
for us I think that means the neutrality of the Internet.
Let's make the Internet open, lower the price of
infrastructure, and give people even more freedom in the
way they use it. That is the first goal. I proposed this at
the Industrial Competitiveness Council within my IT
autobahn concept, which I've talked about before.
Information and communications technology
infrastructure should be nationalized, and we should
create the world's fastest and cheapest communications
environment. It should be free and open to everyone.
Furthermore, because there are a lot of applications for
such a system, we need to fight to completely eliminate
any regulations that would hinder those applications.

Ryoichi: That is the duty of the Japan Association of New
Economy, right?

Hiroshi: My basic recognition is that Japanese people
possess competitiveness and are excellent workers.
The social system in Japan is put together well, too.
The problem is either the regulations hindering our
competitiveness or the unique frameworks, standards, and
laws we have here. It's crucial that we eliminate these
hindrances somehow and put our economic metabolism
back on track. I believe that if we liberalize economic
activities and set that economic metabolism back in
motion, competitiveness in Japan will increase on its own.

Ryoichi: You mean that competitiveness will rise even if we
don't do anything beyond that?

Hiroshi: I've said it again and again, but the fact is that
most of the industries that the Ministry of Economy,
Trade and Industry have "contributed" to have all gone

to hell. This has been true of industries that have been overprotected, like home electronics or semiconductors, and it's true of industries where the regulations have been too strict, like the aviation industry. All of these industries have lost their competitiveness. We also have very strong industries, like the automobile industry, that have seen their international competitiveness explode.

Ryoichi: What do you think the strengths of Japanese people are?

Hiroshi: We are serious and we work well in teams. I also think we're highly ethical. We have the ability to accept many different cultures, and we are highly skilled at reconstructing those cultures to create hybrid products. Just look at things like ramen, which is the Japanized version of Chinese noodle soups, or our "curry rice," where we managed to create an entirely new type of food through innovations with Indian curries. We take in a lot of cultures, and we mix them—they don't just come here and exist in isolation from each other. I think that is the strength of Japan.

Ryoichi: I'm of the same opinion. Japan has been developing this way ever since the Meiji Restoration, and I think this aspect of our culture is why we have progressed as much as we have. There are weak points to that, too, but Japan always puts its strongest foot forward. Up to this point, we have consumed a lot of the cultures and technology of Western Europe in a Japanese way. From here on out, I believe that we shouldn't hesitate to promote our own culture and technology to people overseas. Japanese people need to cultivate a mentality of being able to do things even if they seem a little brazen. I personally believe it is very important that Japanese people change and become able to say with confidence, "This is what I believe."

Competitiveness as a Platform

Hiroshi: The reason why I am calling this book *The Power to Compete* relates to something that I said during the meeting of the Industrial Competitiveness Council. To have competition, you must have people to compete with. Who are we competing with? The answer to that is the United States, China, South Korea, and the European Union. Competition does not mean warfare. It means being economically superior to other nations when it comes to matters such as the development of products, cost, and sales.

Ryoichi: Competition, in a single sentence, is the basis of a free economy. In economics, when we consider whether an economy has reached perfect equilibrium in terms of free competition, for example, we first consider consumers and corporations as separate units and build our hypotheses from there. In reality, we need to pay attention to the fact that the economy comprises many complex entities, including states, multinational corporations, and industries.

Hiroshi: My priority has been the competitiveness of the state platform. States are platforms comprising many different factors.

Ryoichi: Corporations in the United States have the state at their backs. That platform, in that case, is very important. This relates, for example, to what we talked about earlier [Chapter 7].

Hiroshi: By which I assume you mean, even if the price is a little higher, people will buy goods and services that they associate with the Japanese brand.

Ryoichi: They trust it.

Hiroshi: In which case, it may be good to think about quantitative markers of competitiveness like GDP and employment separately from qualitative markers like branding and trust.

Ryoichi: After World War II, there was faith in the idea that German products were a step above the rest. The best automobiles back then were made by Mercedes Benz and Volkswagen. This extended even to things like pencil sharpeners. It was said that German products produced a good shave, they were sturdily made, and they lasted a long time. I thought that way. Everyone thought that way. Similarly, the faith that the people of China and Southeast Asia have in the Made in Japan brand is very important.

Hiroshi: Looked at as a whole, competiveness is important to the state platform, to capital, to employment, to culture, and to branding. For instance, when a new entrepreneur is thinking about where to create a new company, where they decide to place that company says a lot about that country's competitiveness. If people prioritize Japan, it means we are competitive, but if they choose to build their company in Singapore, it means our competiveness is low.

Ryoichi: As we approach an era in which products are purchased on the Internet, I suppose that goods will begin to sell more on the basis of their brand than on their quality or price. You're actually selling products over the Internet. What do you think about that?

Hiroshi: I think a product's quality and price are important. I think brand power is equally important.

Ryoichi: After all, brand power means the power that you have to instill trust in your customers. People need to be careful about branding.

Hiroshi: In that sense, I think we all need to work together as Team Japan and support the branding of Japan as a whole.

The Global Logistics Revolution

Hiroshi: One thing that I am curious about is corporations within Japan that are trying out new things. I don't think very many companies here have a founder or owner who is leading the company toward growth, which is a model that we see a lot in the United States. I wish the leaders of Japanese companies would take management a bit more seriously. Even if it's someone who's a leader through and through and promoted up from the ranks of the administrative staff, I just wish we had more leaders with the courage to give something a go for the sake of their own company. [laughs] During the period of high growth, we had people like that—presidents promoted up from administrative positions who managed like they owned the companies they worked at.

    I think that, given the lifetime employment system, the only company presidents we can hope for are people who have been promoted up through the company. The standard model is no good. The head coach of the Tohoku Rakuten Golden Eagles is Senichi Hoshino. He used to play for the Chunichi Dragons. So what? [laughs] I think the only teams who care about having their coaches come from within their own clubs are the Giants and Hiroshima.

Ryoichi: That sort of Japanese corporate culture—or you might call it corporate structure—worries me.

Hiroshi: To take that further, I think people have the strong sense that it is a loss if a foreign company buys up a Japanese company, but the feeling overseas is the opposite. When Rakuten once bought a Canadian company, the Canadian government thanked us. They went nearly as far as proclaiming us Canadians from that day forward.

It was the same way in France. Some time ago, the French government informed me that I was to receive the National Order of the Legion of Honour for my contributions to job creation there. It's a traditional award that dates back to the time of Napoleon, and it is given to people who contribute to the French state.

Ryoichi: You don't say? That's great. Congratulations. We need to celebrate! [laughs]

Hiroshi: And that's why I think we need to change the way that people feel about acquisitions here. I also think we need to do something about defensive measures that protect companies from acquisition. They should be more open as well.

Ryoichi: I think it's fine for companies to defend themselves, but it should be done in a fair and open manner, and the companies that defend themselves and end up the better for it must publicize that.

Hiroshi: Recently, there has been a lot of debate about business-to-business interactions, and I think we will reach an era when business-to-consumer interactions become important for trade theory.

For example, right now digital content on DVDs and CDs and so on is mainly only being distributed in Japan, but I think we will see more downloads from servers overseas in the near future. The same thing may happen for financial services. A lot of people are talking about cloud computing right now, and they are making that shift to the cloud, too. In other words, I think we have reached a point where we are about to see an era of direct purchases from overseas sources by individuals. Once we enter that era, trade will no longer be something that we talk about as happening solely among companies. It will instead come to be tremendously affected by consumer trends. And when that happens, we will need to really give a lot of thought to how consumer behaviors are changing if we want to succeed.

For instance, I think less than 30 percent of the clothes we wear today are made in Japan. Seventy percent are products of China or other countries in Asia. Right now, domestic corporations are importing the products made overseas and selling them here, but it would be faster and cheaper if we could buy the products directly from the manufacturers. In other words, there is going to be a global distribution revolution. And knowing that, we shouldn't be working to prevent it; we should be thinking about how we can jump ahead and profit from it while other countries are still hesitating. To that end, too, it is vital that we work to eliminate regulations. I believe that this country has high-quality citizens; I believe that we should have confidence in our superior, competitive position; and I believe that we must actively promote liberalization.

Ryoichi: As long as Japan is a trading nation, we will need competiveness in order to succeed. The major point here is how we create that competitiveness. We are talking about an abstract concept, but we need the people of this nation to understand competiveness and support Japan. To make that happen, it is crucial that we have a good flow of information, including over the Internet, and I would hope that the mass media will work hard to help us with this.

Hiroshi: As we work toward that, we shouldn't try to go it alone. I think it's very important that we create a Japan that is attractive to foreign nationals as part of our efforts to create a platform that will draw many different races and nationalities here. It doesn't matter who is active *in* Japan—whether they be foreign nationals or foreign corporations—as long as they are active *for* Japan. We must first create an attractive country, a platform, if we are ever going to draw superior minds to Japan and see a future in which many more innovative experiments are being done here.

Summary

- Deregulate and bring the power to compete back to Japan.
- Utilize the strengths of Japan, which is a cultural melting pot.
- Take the lead in the global logistics revolution and actively seek opportunities.
- Create an economic platform that positions Japan as a country attractive to foreign nationals.

Epilogue

"Boys, be ambitious!" William S. Clark, a teacher at Sapporo Agricultural College [now Hokkaido University], is famous for leaving his students with these words of encouragement.

As if answering Dr. Clark's call to action, a great many ambitious young people came to gather around Sapporo at the start of the Meiji period. One such person was Inazo Nitobe, the man now depicted on the 5,000-yen note, but I don't think that many Japanese people know what Nitobe accomplished.

Nitobe was born in a warrior household of the southern Morioka domain. He studied at Sapporo Agricultural College alongside people like Kanzo Uchimura and others, and, at the age of 21, he set a grand life goal of becoming a bridge between nations across the Pacific Ocean. He quit a course at Imperial University midway through to go study abroad in the United States. He studied in Germany after that, and then he took a position at his alma mater, Sapporo Agricultural College, upon returning to Japan. In 1900, while he was still in the United States, he authored *Bushido: The Soul of Japan* in English. The book became a best-seller. It was translated into German, French, and other languages, and read around the world.

Following his time teaching at Sapporo Agricultural College, Nitobe moved on to other positions, including

professor at Kyoto Imperial University and principal of First
Higher School, Japan, before finally settling into a position
as an undersecretary-general of the League of Nations. In
that capacity, he traveled around the world giving lectures,
charming people like Albert Einstein and Marie Curie, and
eventually establishing the International Committee on Intellectual Cooperation, an organization that would later come to
be known as the United Nations Educational, Scientific and
Cultural Organization.

Nitobe, along with Yukichi Fukuzawa, the founder of
Keio University, and others, was part of what could be called
the first generation of intellectual elite in Japan following the
Meiji Restoration. They were people with wide perspectives
of the world beyond the seas—people who thought about
things in global terms. I strongly wish that we would see the
emergence of many people like Nitobe from among today's
Japanese youth.

If we did, and if I were asked to give advice to someone
like that, I would caution them about one thing: Globalization does not mean losing your nationality. The world now
requires that we speak English. This is only natural, but we
need to understand that true globalization is based on the
precedent that we maintain our identity as Japanese. Take the
good parts of Japan—our history and traditions—into your
work on the international stage. In doing so, you will make
a contribution to the world.

I have always enjoyed debate. It was a tremendous joy to
be able to hold such grand discussions this time on so many
different themes with my son Hiroshi. I cannot imagine that
many fathers get to debate with their sons like this, and from
that perspective, I think of it as a great honor. I can only hope
that this father-and-son conversation will be of some benefit
to the young people of Japan as they work on the international
stage and become true global leaders.

I want to express my gratitude to my wife, Setsuko, who helped organize our materials and took care of me, as well as my children and grandchildren. And I also want to say thank you to Hiroshi one more time for making this opportunity possible. Thank you so much. Know that I pray from the bottom of my heart that you will continue to work so hard for our country's global development.

Ryoichi Mikitani
Professor Emeritus
Kobe University
August 2013

Acknowledgments

Many people contributed to the creation of this book and I would like to take this opportunity to acknowledge them and thank them for their efforts.

Quite a few Rakuten members contributed their time, skill, and hard work to this manuscript. Thank you to the CEO Office, Global Marketing, and PR teams, and to all the executives who contributed their time and effort in interviews and other critical tasks.

I would also like to thank those who came from outside Rakuten to join in the effort of bringing this book into being. Firstly, thank you to Kodansha for the original Japanese publication of *The Power to Compete*. Thank you to my agent, Leah Spiro of Riverside Creative Management, for her guidance. Thank you to Shannon Vargo and her team at John Wiley & Sons for believing in the project and guiding it through the publishing experience. Thanks also to Ellen Neuborne and Diane Aronson for their help in the editing process.

Thank you to everyone who is encouraging innovation and fighting to make Japan, and the world, a better place for future generations.

Finally, thank you to my family for their inspiration and support.

And to mother and father, thank you for all the knowledge, wisdom, and guidance you have shared with me over the years.

Index